Canada's
Wilderness Lands

Prepared by the Special Publications Division

National Geographic Society, Washington, D.C.

Canada's Wilderness Lands

Published by
  The National Geographic Society
  GILBERT M. GROSVENOR, *President*
  MELVIN M. PAYNE, *Chairman of the Board*
  OWEN R. ANDERSON, *Executive Vice President*
  ROBERT L. BREEDEN, *Vice President, Publications
    and Educational Media*

Prepared by
  The Special Publications Division
  DONALD J. CRUMP, *Editor*
  PHILIP B. SILCOTT, *Associate Editor*
  WILLIAM L. ALLEN, WILLIAM R. GRAY, *Senior Editors*

Staff for this book
  PAUL D. MARTIN, *Managing Editor*
  THOMAS B. POWELL III, *Picture Editor*
  SUEZ B. KEHL, *Art Director*
  STEPHEN J. HUBBARD, BARBARA A. PAYNE, *Senior Researchers*
  JENNIFER C. URQUHART, *Project Coordinator*

Illustrations and Design
  MARIANNE R. KOSZORUS, *Design Assistant*
  JOHN D. GARST, JR., PETER J. BALCH, SUSANAH B. BROWN,
    JUDITH BELL SIEGEL, *Map Research, Design, and Production*
  LOUIS DE LA HABA, RON FISHER, CHRISTINE ECKSTROM LEE,
    JANE R. McCAULEY, THOMAS O'NEILL, *Picture Legend Writers*

Engraving, Printing, and Product Manufacture
  ROBERT W. MESSER, *Manager;* GEORGE V. WHITE, *Production Manager;* GREGORY STORER, *Production Project Manager*
  MARK R. DUNLEVY, RICHARD A. McCLURE, DAVID V. SHOWERS, *Assistant Production Managers*
  KATHERINE H. DONOHUE, *Senior Production Assistant;* MARY A. BENNETT, *Production Assistant;* KATHERINE R. LEITCH,
  Production Staff Assistant

NANCY F. BERRY, PAMELA A. BLACK, NETTIE BURKE, MARY ELIZABETH DAVIS, CLAIRE M. DOIG, ROSAMUND GARNER, VICTORIA
  D. GARRETT, MARY JANE GORE, JANE R. HALPIN, NANCY J. HARVEY, SHERYL A. HOEY, JOAN HURST, ARTEMIS S. LAMPATHAKIS,
  VIRGINIA A. McCOY, MERRICK P. MURDOCK, CLEO PETROFF, VICTORIA I. PISCOPO, TAMMY PRESLEY, CAROL A. ROCHELEAU,
  KATHERYN M. SLOCUM, JENNY TAKACS, *Staff Assistants;* CAROLE L. TYLER, *Intern*

MICHAEL G. YOUNG, *Index*

*Sunset ignites sea and sky in Rocky Harbour, Newfoundland, where herring gulls perch on exposed boulders at low tide. Preceding pages:
Rafters pole the rippled waters of Pinto Lake, in western Alberta. Snow-dusted peaks of the Rocky Mountains tower above the far shore.
Page 1: Displaying a magnificent rack, a caribou of the George River herd treads the barrens of northern Quebec. Six major caribou herds
wander the wilderness lands of Canada. Hardcover: A red maple leaf, Canada's colorful national emblem.*

YVA MOMATIUK AND JOHN EASTCOTT; SAM ABELL, PRECEDING PAGES; RICHARD A. COOKE III, PAGE 1 AND HARDCOVER.

Foreword

EVER SINCE I WAS A BOY, I have considered myself part Canadian. I recall hearing stories of how, in 1870, my family emigrated from Scotland to Ontario to take advantage of the invigorating climate. For the past 80 years five generations of my family have summered in Baddeck, Nova Scotia, at the house built by my great-grandfather, Alexander Graham Bell, one of the founders of the National Geographic Society. I think of my early years, and I remember hiking along magnificent sea cliffs on Cape Breton Island, or of learning to sail on Bras d'Or Lake and cruising in the deep blue coves and bays of that beautiful shoreline.

Since my boyhood, I have traveled widely through Canada. I have ridden horses high into the Rocky Mountains in Jasper National Park, driven every mile of the Trans-Canada Highway between Sydney and Vancouver, sailed the spectacular Inside Passage along the west coast, and flown across the high Arctic from the Beaufort Sea to Ellesmere Island and north to the North Pole. People invariably ask me which experience I most enjoyed, and I always have to answer that I liked them all, because each one was unique. My answer, I now realize, testifies to the great variety—and overwhelming size—of the Canadian wilderness. Two-thirds of Canada lies in an undeveloped state. If you translate this area to the United States, you would have to imagine a wilderness stretching from the Rocky Mountains to the Atlantic seaboard.

Once, when I was flying near the Beaufort Sea, I looked down and saw a herd of caribou crossing from the Yukon Territory into Alaska. This natural, unimpeded movement across the boundaries of two countries has come to symbolize for me the special partnership that exists between Canada and the United States. The National Geographic Society recognizes and promotes this friendship. One of the Society's long-standing concerns has been the protection of wilderness. In 1979 we watched with pleasure as the United Nations designated an area in the Wrangell-St. Elias Mountains, on the Yukon-Alaska border, as a world heritage site. The Society has also paid vigilant attention to the environmental risks involved in the construction of a natural gas pipeline from the Arctic to southern Canada and the United States: The health of the Canadian wilderness remains among our vital interests.

For the past several years I have observed the admirable measures Canada has taken to preserve its scenic lands. Balancing resource development with sound conservation, the Canadian government has established 11 new national parks since 1968, protecting for all future generations incomparable landscapes of ice fields, deep canyons, white-water rivers, alpine meadows, and thundering waterfalls.

Canada's Wilderness Lands celebrates such treasures. I dedicate this book to the citizens of Canada, in recognition of their magnificent natural heritage, and to the citizens of the United States, that they may come to know better those wild and beautiful lands.

Gilbert M. Grosvenor, President
National Geographic Society

Bulling his way through thigh-deep water, a moose with velvet-covered antlers splashes across the Thelon River, in the Northwest Territories.
RICHARD A. COOKE III

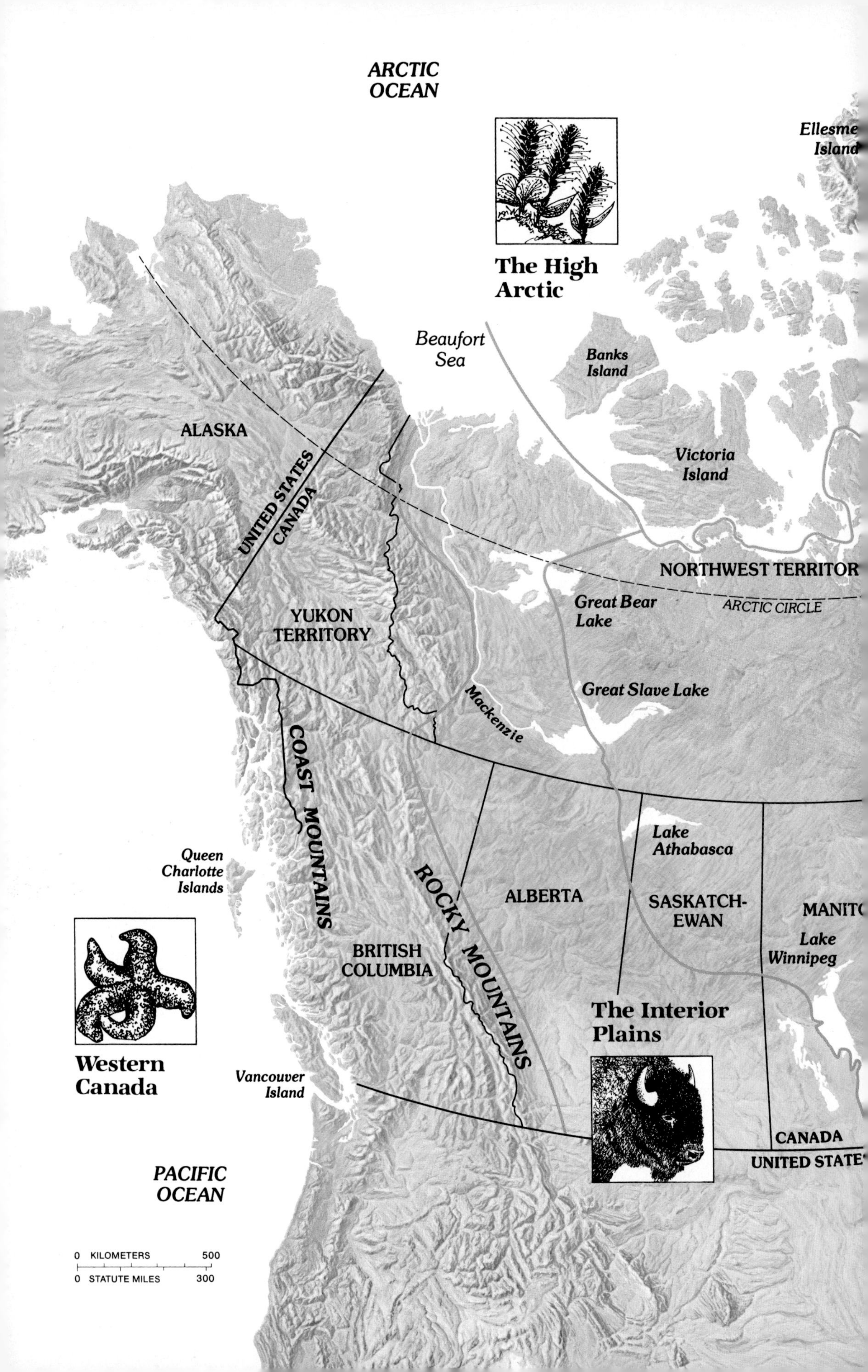

ARCTIC
OCEAN

**The High
Arctic**

*Ellesme
Island*

*Beaufort
Sea*

*Banks
Island*

ALASKA

*Victoria
Island*

UNITED STATES
CANADA

NORTHWEST TERRITOR

*Great Bear
Lake*

ARCTIC CIRCLE

YUKON
TERRITORY

Great Slave Lake

Mackenzie

COAST MOUNTAINS

*Queen
Charlotte
Islands*

*Lake
Athabasca*

ROCKY MOUNTAINS

ALBERTA

SASKATCH-
EWAN

MANITO

BRITISH
COLUMBIA

*Lake
Winnipeg*

**The Interior
Plains**

**Western
Canada**

*Vancouver
Island*

CANADA

UNITED STATE

PACIFIC
OCEAN

| 0 | KILOMETERS | 500 |
| 0 | STATUTE MILES | 300 |

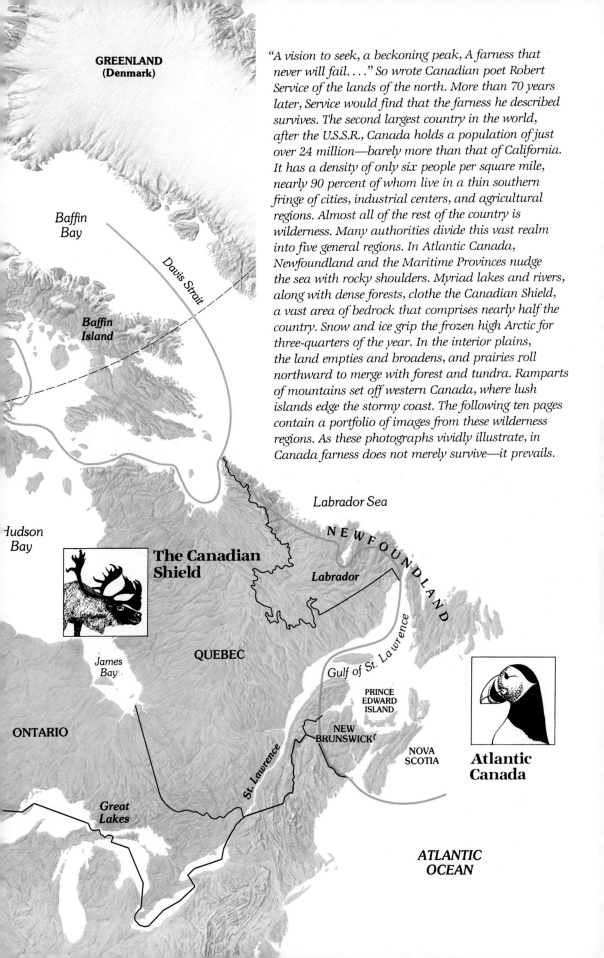

GREENLAND
(Denmark)

"A vision to seek, a beckoning peak, A farness that never will fail...." So wrote Canadian poet Robert Service of the lands of the north. More than 70 years later, Service would find that the farness he described survives. The second largest country in the world, after the U.S.S.R., Canada holds a population of just over 24 million—barely more than that of California. It has a density of only six people per square mile, nearly 90 percent of whom live in a thin southern fringe of cities, industrial centers, and agricultural regions. Almost all of the rest of the country is wilderness. Many authorities divide this vast realm into five general regions. In Atlantic Canada, Newfoundland and the Maritime Provinces nudge the sea with rocky shoulders. Myriad lakes and rivers, along with dense forests, clothe the Canadian Shield, a vast area of bedrock that comprises nearly half the country. Snow and ice grip the frozen high Arctic for three-quarters of the year. In the interior plains, the land empties and broadens, and prairies roll northward to merge with forest and tundra. Ramparts of mountains set off western Canada, where lush islands edge the stormy coast. The following ten pages contain a portfolio of images from these wilderness regions. As these photographs vividly illustrate, in Canada farness does not merely survive—it prevails.

Baffin Bay

Davis Strait

Baffin Island

Labrador Sea

NEWFOUNDLAND

Hudson Bay

The Canadian Shield

Labrador

QUEBEC

James Bay

Gulf of St. Lawrence

PRINCE EDWARD ISLAND

ONTARIO

NEW BRUNSWICK

NOVA SCOTIA

St. Lawrence

Atlantic Canada

Great Lakes

ATLANTIC OCEAN

ATLANTIC CANADA: Brooding clouds darken Saglek Bay, a deep slash in the rock-strewn

coast of northern Labrador. The jagged Torngat Mountains rise in the background.

THE CANADIAN SHIELD: Up from the depths of the continent's foundation, outcroppings

RICHARD A. COOKE III

of ancient Precambrian rock pierce an autumn-tinted slope in southern Quebec.

13

THE HIGH ARCTIC: August snow shrouds the skull of a musk-ox lying in bleak

isolation on Banks Island, westernmost isle in the sweeping Arctic Archipelago.

THE INTERIOR PLAINS: *Stillness enfolds a virgin mixed-grass prairie in southeastern*

Alberta. The Sweet Grass Hills of Montana float mirage-like on the horizon.

WESTERN CANADA: *Along the wild Pacific coast, gulls and cormorants stand raucous*

SAM ABELL

guard above basking sea lions. Here, abundant food sources nurture a wealth of life.

19

Atlantic Canada

Text and Photographs by Yva Momatiuk and John Eastcott

Glacier-chiseled cliffs rim Western Brook Pond, in Newfoundland's Gros Morne National Park. Gros Morne evokes the beauty of Atlantic Canada, realm of rugged mountains and wind-lashed shores.

Atlantic Canada

"WHALES!" MY HEAD SPUN AROUND. Two minke whales breached, glistening indigo in the late sun. The whales sounded and surfaced again as if lured by the June light. Our 22-month-old daughter, Tara, cried in her clear voice: "Big fish!" and watched the great marine mammals. My husband, John, came aft. The fishing boat moved on, hugging the west coast of the Island of Newfoundland and churning the waters of the Gulf of St. Lawrence.

The small talk did not resume; the whales had cast their spell. They were very close, perhaps feeding beneath us or following in our wake. We watched each wave grow, hoping it would part suddenly with a foamy swoosh to reveal the slow, cartwheeling motion of a huge, muscular back.

Although hunted and admired for centuries, whales remain largely a mystery. Their lives and deaths, their songs and calls, their long travels all belong to the dark abyss of the sea. Is that fleeting glimpse of these creatures so thrilling because they are among the largest animals that have ever lived? Whatever its source, this thrill did not diminish throughout the summer we spent exploring the wilderness of Atlantic Canada. During more than three months, we were to journey from the Maritimes to the rugged Torngat Mountains of northern Labrador, and the sea was never far away.

The whales did not reappear that day. At dusk our boat returned to Rocky Harbour, a fishing village scattered north of Newfoundland's Bonne Bay. The great flat-topped mass of 2,644-foot Gros Morne shelters the village from easterly gales and gives its name to Gros Morne National Park, the first stop in our travels.

Set aside by the Canadian government in 1973, Gros Morne National Park encompasses a section of rugged shoreline along the gulf, an area of coastal lowlands, and a part of the Long Range Mountains—a high plateau that parallels the coast. Glaciers long ago scoured Gros Morne, shearing off upland peaks, plowing out giant fiords, and leaving behind boulders and innumerable ponds that shine dully like pewter plates. The park has been suggested for nomination as a world heritage site, a designation given by the United Nations to areas of great significance to all mankind. If its nomination is approved, Gros Morne will join the list of such famous sites as the Galapagos Islands and the Grand Canyon.

Except for a few trails inside the park's boundaries, this 750-square-mile chunk of wilderness remains undeveloped. Much of it is made almost inaccessible by a low, nearly impenetrable thicket of balsam fir and black spruce, known locally as "tuckamore." Pruned by wind and frost, tuckamore grows by the sea and on the steep sides of the plateau. As Dave Huddlestone, the assistant park interpreter, explained, "For hiking through 'tuck' you need a machete, a chain saw, and a bag of peanuts."

"Peanuts? To bribe bears?" I guessed brightly.

"No, for energy."

In wind-sheltered valleys of the park, boreal forests of balsam fir, spruce, and birch grow thickly. The forests shelter foxes, otters, black bears, and moose. The windswept highlands belong to hard winters, rock ptarmigans, caribou, and big arctic hares.

John and I quickly discovered one of Gros Morne's most distinguishing features—its weather. Embraced by the frigid Labrador Current, the Island of Newfoundland is known for foul gales,

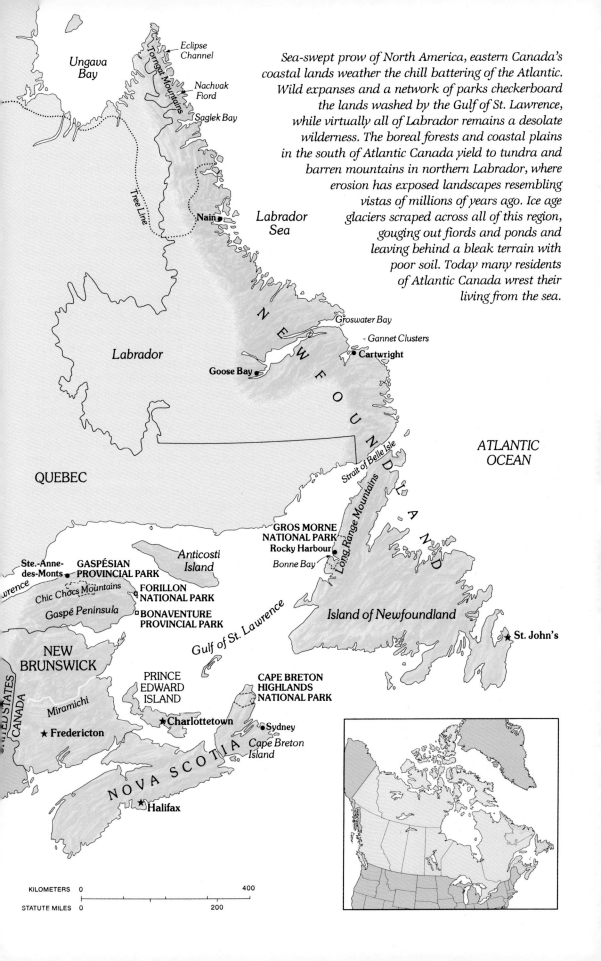

Ungava
Bay

Eclipse
Channel

Nachvak
Fiord

Saglek Bay

Torngat Mountains

Tree Line

• Nain

Labrador
Sea

Labrador

Sea-swept prow of North America, eastern Canada's
coastal lands weather the chill battering of the Atlantic.
Wild expanses and a network of parks checkerboard
the lands washed by the Gulf of St. Lawrence,
while virtually all of Labrador remains a desolate
wilderness. The boreal forests and coastal plains
in the south of Atlantic Canada yield to tundra and
barren mountains in northern Labrador, where
erosion has exposed landscapes resembling
vistas of millions of years ago. Ice age
glaciers scraped across all of this region,
gouging out fiords and ponds and
leaving behind a bleak terrain with
poor soil. Today many residents
of Atlantic Canada wrest their
living from the sea.

Groswater Bay

Gannet Clusters

• Cartwright

Goose Bay •

N E W F O U N D L A N D

ATLANTIC
OCEAN

QUEBEC

Strait of Belle Isle

Long Range Mountains

GROS MORNE
NATIONAL PARK
Rocky Harbour •

Anticosti
Island

Bonne Bay

Ste.-Anne-
des-Monts

GASPÉSIAN
PROVINCIAL PARK

Lawrence

Chic Chocs Mountains

FORILLON
NATIONAL PARK

Gaspé Peninsula

BONAVENTURE
PROVINCIAL PARK

Gulf of St. Lawrence

Island of Newfoundland

★ St. John's

NEW
BRUNSWICK

PRINCE
EDWARD
ISLAND

CAPE BRETON
HIGHLANDS
NATIONAL PARK

Miramichi

UNITED STATES
CANADA

★ Charlottetown

• Sydney
Cape Breton
Island

★ Fredericton

N O V A   S C O T I A

★ Halifax

KILOMETERS   0   400

STATUTE MILES   0   200

driving rain, thick fog, and rapid weather changes. Its location at the eastern extremity of North America subjects it to both oceanic and continental weather systems. After several days of rain and numerous fat lobsters boiled in seawater, I suggested to John, "Let's ask Dave Huddlestone to come with us to Green Point."

"In this weather?" said John.

"Maybe it never clears in Newfoundland," I said. "Remember Captain Cook's account of his six summers here?" While surveying these waters Cook used to anchor in Bonne Bay, often immobilized by "much rain and thick fog," or by "strong gales and hard rain."

Dave, however, did agree to come with us, and we set out for Green Point, one of the prominent coastal headlands in the park. Where the headland juts out into the gulf, layers of rock stand on end, resembling tattered books. Dave stopped and intoned as if speaking for the rocks above us, "We were once the edge of the continent but we were underwater. Layers of sediment were laid down upon us. . . ." Gros Morne is a living lesson in geology. Scientists theorize that the continents were once a single landmass. As the centuries passed, this landmass broke apart, and the continents separated and collided as they drifted over the earth's surface.

One such collision, beginning some 400 million years ago, produced the Appalachian Mountains system; Newfoundland's Long Range lies at the northernmost end. The Long Range was formed as pressure from the colliding continents uplifted masses of sedimentary rock to the top of the present coastal plain. The edge of the plain, ravaged by wind and sea, has been breaking up into coves, beaches, and headlands ever since. Green Point reveals a network of folded layers, with rows of bulges called *boudinage*, a French word for strings of sausages. We walked, touched, and looked.

Dave smiled. "Geologists can really lose their heads in Gros Morne," he said.

Gros Morne's fiords and ponds offer striking evidence of the erosive power of glaciers. During the last ice age, massive ice sheets crept down from the Arctic region to cover much of North America. Over most of Atlantic Canada, the ice stripped away the soil, creating a rocky, infertile land whose later inhabitants would have to turn to the sea for their livelihood.

Summer's blush, a dainty Virginia rose adds a splash of hot color to a coastal plain in northern Nova Scotia's Cape Breton Highlands National Park.

One day we followed a park trail to Western Brook Pond, retracing the path of those long-vanished rivers of ice over the coastal plains. The bog here sparkled with orchids, blue irises, and the red goblets of pitcher plants. Little Tara bounded on the peat moss. Bees hummed. At Western Brook Pond we found a ten-mile-long, twisted wind tunnel of a canyon. Waterfalls jumped free from the plateau 2,000 feet above, and gulls nested among the crags. Local people still remember how years ago a whole cliff face collapsed into the pond. One of the park employees told us, "It is beautiful, but I don't like being there. Look up, and you'll see deep cracks in the cliffs. One day it will go again. In the winter even a small pebble from the top can crack the thick ice of the pond."

Another afternoon, at low tide, we went to the coast to slosh through tidal pools with Rob Walker, the park's chief interpreter. Rob is an intense man, as if living close to nature keeps him constantly alert. The pools we saw sheltered creatures that were either small or secretive, or both. But a careful search revealed blue mussels, rock crabs, blossoms of sea anemones, and hermit crabs, looking uncomfortable in their borrowed shells.

Rob pointed to a group of periwinkles. "They are vegetarian snails. They lick algae off the rocks with sharp, rasping tongues. And here is their predator, a meat-eating snail called dog whelk." Rob picked up two sea urchins, flattened globes of fused plates covered with spikes. "They eat the bait out of lobster traps. Fishermen hate them. Yet fishing for cod and halibut depleted the very species that prey on sea urchins. And now sea urchins are devouring the kelp beds that are the spawning grounds for fish."

Rob reminded us of the importance of fishing to Canada. "Fishing is our oldest industry. It was the cod, lobster, haddock, flounder, herring, mackerel, and salmon that drew settlers from the Old World." More than half of Canada's annual fish harvest of two and a half billion pounds comes from the Atlantic Provinces.

Near the end of our stay in Gros Morne, we visited the sea-blue frame house of Annie Walters, in Rocky Harbour. At the entrance to the bay in Rocky Harbour a lighthouse warns against submerged rocks, aptly called "sunkers" in Newfoundland. Annie watches the light from her house. The lighthouse was her home when she was a child, and now she is 86 years old.

"Even after I married and moved away from home, the last thing I did each night was look at the light," she said in her small but clear voice. Annie's years have stooped her shoulders but have given her memories as vivid as spring flowers. "If the light wasn't on I would call Pop. 'What's the trouble?' I'd ask. Even now I feel that the light is my responsibility." Behind Annie's chair homemade woolen socks hung around the kitchen range.

"Sit here so I can hear you," she said. "Where are you from?"

"Poland," I answered, and felt it could have been the moon.

"Poland? Much in the news now. Hasn't been in years. We used to make socks, gloves, and pies. Sent them over during the war, through the Red Cross."

They did? But the people here were poor, too, eking out a living from the sea and the forest. Even now Newfoundland has one of the lowest per capita incomes in Canada. I felt warmly grateful.

Some years ago Annie was invited to a music festival in Newport, Rhode Island, to sing Newfoundland folk songs. I asked when she had learned to sing. "Once a year Pop used to go caribou hunting, and Mom tended the light," said Annie. "She sang day and night to keep awake, afraid the light might go out."

"Would you sing for us?" I asked. Annie nodded. It was a ballad about sealers stranded on wind-driven ice.

They wove their hands in wild despair/And did for rescue pray,
But not a soul was near to help/That freezing winter day.
Alone within the lighthouse tower/The keeper's wife did see
Her loved ones carried to their doom/Toward the open sea. . . .

AT THE END OF JUNE we flew over the open sea north of the Strait of Belle Isle. We were on our way to Labrador, where in March, on ice floes called The Front, snowy harp seal pups are born. Three weeks of incessant suckling of ultrarich mothers' milk turns the baby seals into blubber-lined, formidable swimming and fishing machines. They will swim north, following the *(Continued on page 32)*

Ghost forest by the sea: Bleached skeletons of balsam firs rise from ten-foot-high dunes in Gros Morne National Park, along Newfoundland's western shore. Blustery winds stunt the hardy trees that grow on Canada's coastal plains; sands blown inland can engulf and destroy the seaside woodlands.

Jumbled boulders litter the Tableland, a high plateau in Gros Morne National Park. This 62-square-mile massif formed from molten magma deep under the ocean floor. Uplifted millions of years ago, the Tableland offers a rare glimpse of the contact between the earth's mantle and crust. A shattered boulder atop the Tableland (below) reveals veined green layers of the metamorphic mineral serpentine. The Tableland's soil supports only a few species of arctic and alpine plants. An old saying about nearby Labrador befits this forbidding land as well: "God made Labrador in six days. And on the seventh, He threw stones at it."

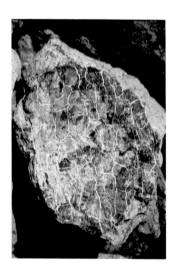

Frothy stream tumbles down the windswept palisades of Western
Brook Pond, in Gros Morne. Sheer cliffs tower 2,000 feet above the
former fiord: As glaciers receded, a rising coastal plain cut access to
the sea, creating the present freshwater pond. The soggy coastlands
of Gros Morne sustain plants adapted to survive in a nutrient-
poor environment, such as the flashy bog laurel (above), on which
a crab spider rests. Fertile fishing grounds first drew settlers to
eastern Canada nearly four centuries ago. Cod fishermen in the Gulf
of St. Lawrence (top) face the rigors of the sea in a motorized dory.

Just dropping in, a trio of puffins lands on one of the Gannet Clusters, a group of rocky isles in

Labrador's Groswater Bay. Thousands of puffins and other seabirds gather here in summer to nest.

Touching the lives of the ancients, archaeologist Callum Thomson examines an artifact discovered at an island site in Labrador's Saglek Bay. An arctic people called the Dorset once occupied the site. Part of a culture known as the Arctic Small Tool tradition, the Dorset people thrived for some 2,000 years. Around A.D. 1400 they vanished from Labrador— replaced by people of the Thule culture. At bottom, Thomson holds the Dorset artifact—a soapstone carving that may portray one of the early Thule hunters to reach this area.

receding ice to the Arctic Archipelago. That is, if they live that long. Soon after they are born, ships bring men with clubs and sharp "sculping" knives. The men are after the pups, or "whitecoats."

Since fishing is a seasonal occupation in this region, spring sealing has traditionally had great importance for the people of Newfoundland. For more than a century sealers have harvested the white pelts. In the early years of sealing, in the late 1800s and early 1900s, thousands of half-starved men risked their lives on the moving spring ice for meager wages paid by their shipmasters. Hundreds of sealers froze or drowned. Even now Canada's sealers often come from impoverished fishing villages. Official reports estimate the present harp seal population of Canada at more than one million. The seal harvest is controlled by government quotas, yet both the quotas and the methods of the kill remain highly controversial.

After arriving in Labrador, John and I were stuck in the settlement of Cartwright while trying to find transportation to the Gannet Clusters, a group of islands containing Labrador's largest seabird community. Dr. David Nettleship, a research biologist with the Canadian Wildlife Service, had invited us to join a group of young scientists who were there studying the breeding birds.

If you find a skipper but discover the sea is too rough for travel or locate a plane but can find no fuel—if you are stranded for days between hope and despair—then you just might be in Labrador. But we were lucky. One Cartwright family, Ron and Alfreda Lethbridge, offered us their hospitality.

Cartwright today has some 650 inhabitants. When French explorer Jacques Cartier anchored not far from here in 1534, he wrote, ". . . there is nothing but moss and small stunted woods. In short, I deem . . . that it is the land that God gave to Cain." Not quite. The people here fish, hunt, and trap. At the Lethbridges we feasted on succulent cod tongues, salmon, and partridgeberry pies. Alfreda's larder was full of wild meat.

After several days, we finally cajoled a helicopter pilot to fly us to a deserted island in the Gannet Clusters, a mile away from the study site. The next afternoon, when the scientists' boat came to pick us up, the eight-foot swell was decidedly unfriendly. I held Tara, a little bundle of warmth swaddled in two life jackets. Suddenly small birds with gaudy beaks zoomed past. Puffins!

Fear vanished. It had been John's childhood dream to see puffins, and in the Gannet Clusters there were 33,000 pairs. Their local name is "sea parrot," or "hatchet face." We saw other birds: elegant razorbills, looking like undertakers in black with white piping; murres, much hunted for food; fulmars, or "noddies"; black-legged kittiwakes, strangely known as "tickle-asses." But despite the islands' name, there were no gannets; the islands are said to have been named in the late 1800s after a British survey vessel.

A small cove sheltered our landing. We met the scientists working on the study island, pitched our tent, and went bird-watching. I carefully crawled up a gully that was riddled with nesting burrows dug by puffins. Up on a rocky ledge, calm in the blowing gale, perched scores of puffins. Some rapped their huge bills together, or kissed the plump cheeks of their mates. Others just pondered. Bright eyes were outlined theatrically in black. Guttural cries of *"ha-aa, ha-aa"* filled the air. Puffins seem happiest in a

crowd, and unlike many other colonial seabirds, they show little aggressiveness. What perfect city dwellers they would make.

Seabirds account for only 3 percent of the world's 8,660 species of birds. Some are superb fliers, while others are flightless. All share a limited ability to walk, but possess great prowess in swimming and feeding in the sea, where they spend most of their lives.

Dr. Tim Birkhead, a research associate of Dr. Nettleship's, told us, "Many murres lay their solitary eggs at the same spot for years. Sometimes they breed on sloping ledges. One pair may incubate its egg for days, carefully exchanging the egg between them with their feet as each takes its turn. Then suddenly one needs to scratch . . . and off rolls the egg."

Dr. Birkhead and other members of the research team spent up to 16 hours a day studying the birds. Such work helps expand basic biological knowledge, but the fate of the seabirds really depends on the needs of humans for living space, food, fuel . . . and profits. Over the years, seabirds have been hunted for their meat and oil; eggs have been taken and breeding grounds disturbed; the birds have been used for fishing bait—and even for fertilizer. Nowadays birds are often accidentally caught in gill nets. Waterborne chemicals can interfere with their ability to reproduce, and oil spills can coat their feathers and kill them.

Some seabirds, such as the great auk, have already become extinct; most others continue to decline in number. We heard one marine biologist lament, "Sometimes I think that we study them so we will know what we lost." Saddened, we shared his fears.

Shortly after we left the seabird colony we were stuck again, this time in Goose Bay, a town in the heart of Labrador. The distance between Goose Bay and the Torngat Mountains, where we had planned to go, is 900 miles round trip, vastly exceeding the range of a bush plane. We would have to refuel in Nain, the northernmost settlement on the coast. But the aviation fuel we had arranged for had been put on the wrong boat and was not there.

"Have you inquired about flying up with Petro-Canada?" asked

Rock-strewn floor of a Dorset dwelling emerges at the Saglek Bay site being investigated by Callum Thomson. Built with rafters of wood or whalebone and covered with animal skins and sod, the partially underground house provided winter shelter for a Dorset family nearly a thousand years ago.

Stu Luttich, a provincial biologist. Stu was referring to the federally owned corporation that is presently conducting oil explorations off Labrador. "They have a base in Saglek Bay at the southern end of the Torngats," said Stu. "It's an old radar and telecommunications station that they use to service their exploratory offshore wells."

Stu hit it right. The next day John and I were able to make special arrangements to join a Petro-Canada flight to Saglek. We flew north, following the coast. Low wetlands and boreal forests gave way to tundra and mountains, which rose directly from the sea. Then we saw the base at Saglek Bay and a man chasing caribou off the landing strip.

Late that evening we went up to the cliffs of Cape Uivak, overlooking the Labrador Sea. With us was Paula Arnet, a 17-year-old friend of ours, and Dave Brown, our guide and a native Labradorian. Paula and Dave had joined us in Goose Bay. Paula recorded in her notes: "Sundown. The mountains are snow-covered, wrapped in bits of golden fog, just as free as ever. Far below, 40 icebergs crowd the bay under the white full moon and the blue-lavender of the sky. It is such an incredible world. . . ."

Flowing south through the Labrador Sea is the Labrador Current, a wide, frigid river referred to as "iceberg alley." The current carries along massive icebergs calved from the glaciers of Greenland and Baffin Island. Fish feed on plankton surrounding the bases of the icebergs; whales and seals follow the fish; and seabirds perch on the glistening ice. Radar and the International Ice Patrol protect ships against the fate of the *Titanic,* but drilling for oil in iceberg alley remains a risky business. Some of Canada's most promising oil and gas resources are in the northern seas, and the technological war against icebergs has just begun.

From Saglek, we planned to fly a hundred miles north to Eclipse Channel. "Why Eclipse?" asked John Andrews, the pilot of our Petro-Canada-chartered helicopter. Well, we had seen a landscape drawing of the area done by a member of an 1860 solar eclipse expedition. The image seemed so unreal that we just had to go there and see the place for ourselves.

The map of the Torngat Mountains shows a tightly drawn maze of contours, indicating the tortuous nature of the terrain. Below us, Cirque Mountain, at 5,144 feet one of the highest peaks of the Torngats, disappeared among countless other snowy crags. There were also red cliffs, razor-sharp ridges, and the shadowy canyons of fiords. The climate of Labrador is considered extremely harsh for its latitude. The yearly mean temperature for this region is below freezing. Nobody lives along this 150-mile range in the north of Labrador, except for Inuit (Eskimos) who come here to fish for arctic char in season. To the Inuit of old, this was Torngarsoak's country. A benevolent god? Or unforgiving, I wondered.

In the helicopter we cruised over Blow Me Down Mountain, Nachvak Fiord, and Big White Bearskin Island. Suddenly the mountains were no longer touching the sea. They were set back in a semicircle, embracing the flattened rubble of the tundra.

"Wow! It looks like the bottom jaw of a shark taking a bite from the sky!" John Andrews exclaimed.

Eclipse. Even as we looked at this giant amphitheater with two dozen separate bastions of gray rock, a sparkling blue bay, and surging waterfalls, it still seemed unreal. The days at Eclipse were to be magical. Caribou grazed undisturbed in brilliant patches of lichens. The sun drew its long summer arc over our camp. Air masses from the land clashed with the icy breath of the sea, and fog would move in, low and golden at sundown. John and I wanted to visit distant valleys, climb the peaks, and never go to sleep. Dave tried to improve the camp and fish for char. Paula, resplendent in her dark summer tan, dreamed. But we did little, as if the Torngats were to be our home forever.

Only Tara worked hard. Her pockets were crammed with wilting flowers, eider duck feathers, even a small caribou bone. She drank from streams like a fawn, collected pebbles, and compared animal droppings. She learned about wind and its force, water and its flow, and one July day she turned two. We had learned from the arctic Inuit some years ago that children flourish in harsh conditions when they feel loved and secure, protected by an extended family. At Eclipse, Tara drew Paula and Dave into ours.

On our last evening at Eclipse, Dave and I sat by the kitchen tent, pitched apart from the sleeping tents to discourage polar bears from visiting us in our beds. We were trying to improve our freeze-dried food by frying it in Dave's salted pork.

Dave was a quiet man, never imposing his views unless he thought our ideas impractical. Although he was 52 years old, his body was powerful and lean, and his strong face evoked his share of Indian blood. Most of the older European settlers in Labrador have some Inuit or Indian ancestors. As we sat by the stove, Dave looked up. Strange clouds emerged and moved rapidly across the sky. I trusted his uncanny understanding of weather.

"What is it going to be, Dave?"

"Do you really want to know?" he joked. I did.

"Wind. A big wind."

That night the wind slammed into our tent. The guy lines pulled taut, vibrating madly. The nylon shell flapped with a deafening noise. Tara dove into my arms. At dawn we folded the tents, throwing our weight on the billowing fabric.

Suddenly we caught the steady whir of the helicopter's blades. John Andrews had made it through.

"A plane might have lost her wings!" he shouted as we loaded our gear. His eyes had the triumphant expression of a boy who knows that he can outrun all others. We flew out of Eclipse, banking sharply and feeling the relentless pounding of the wind. Or was it the Inuit god, Torngarsoak?

A FEW DAYS LATER we were in Cape Breton Highlands National Park, in northern Nova Scotia. The warm Maritime summer, the scores of vacationers, and the highway access to the park, all contrasted sharply with the ruggedness of the Torngats. Yet beyond the beaten tracks we shared the wilderness with only the sturdy few who hiked through the magnificent stands of sugar maple, yellow birch, and beech trees, or climbed the highlands that constitute about 90 percent of the 367-square-mile park.

"This is incredible country," said Dr. Richard Jackson, a geologist who was spending the summer exploring the park's interior with his assistant, Gabrielle Schavran. *(Continued on page 44)*

Deadly charmers, fly amanita mushrooms raise orange caps to the sunshine in Cape Breton Highlands National Park. The showy but poisonous mushrooms contain a substance that proves fatally attractive to black flies—bane of the north.

"It chilled the heart to gaze on these barren lands of Labrador," wrote naturalist John James

Audubon in 1833. Near Eclipse Channel, tundra and bogs stretch to the haunting Torngat peaks.

*Castle of ice drifts past jagged isles along the coast of Labrador
(left). The iceberg's craggy towers reach a hundred feet above the
water. Flowing south from the top of the world, the frigid Labrador
Current carries icebergs calved from arctic glaciers to a slow-melting
end in the warmer waters south of Newfoundland. As sun and sea
erode its surface, the iceberg below will crack, boom, splash, and roll
during its two-to-three-year journey to oblivion. In their promenade
down "iceberg alley," the glittering islands of ice swarm with life: Fish
feed on the plankton near a berg's submerged base; whales may
follow the fish; and thousands of seabirds often pepper the 10 percent
of the iceberg's mass that juts above the sea. Along the shores of
Atlantic Canada, passing icebergs loom as a ghostly reminder of
an age when glaciers gripped and carved the land.*

"These were magical days," say the authors of their midsummer camping journey to Labrador's snow-striped Torngat Mountains. Roughly 250 miles north of Labrador's northernmost settlement, the authors' group pitched tents beside Eclipse Channel (above), site of an 1860 solar eclipse expedition. For several days they savored the land's stark majesty. Belly down, the authors' daughter, Tara, drinks from a snowmelt stream behind the camp; while at Eclipse, Tara celebrated her second birthday. As a cold fog rolls in, guide Dave Brown warms his hands over a small fire. Arctic waters chill the coast, creating a climate in Labrador harsh for its latitude. Even the Inuit establish only seasonal camps along the Torngat shores. Their forefathers revered the range as the home of Torngarsoak, most powerful spirit in their pantheon. South of Eclipse, Mount Razorback soars above Nachvak Fiord (opposite), while countless other crumpled peaks zigzag along the horizon.

Surf's drumbeat thunders against bold headlands on the western shore of Cape Breton Highlands National Park. Most of the nearly 370-square-mile park embraces a mountainous plateau of Acadian forests, bogs, lakes, and barrens. Established in 1936 as the first national park in Atlantic Canada, Cape Breton Highlands preserves a vast wilderness tract within a populated and heavily visited region. One of 45 species of mammals that live in the park, a red fox pauses by the forest's edge (above). Cape Breton also shelters more than 230 species of birds. Cheery bunchberry clusters spangle a woodland floor in the park (below, left), and a sunstruck pitcher plant (below, right)—a primitive insectivore—pokes up from a highland bog.

"As a field geologist I had always wanted to find an area that had never been investigated in great detail, one with ocean and mountains. This is it. The most beautiful world is on top of the highlands. You can actually see bogs being formed and changing over to peat."

We drove to the western side of the highlands and followed Fishing Cove Trail, which descends to the Gulf of St. Lawrence. The going was slippery and slow. Two little green snakes crossed our path. Brilliantly colored mushrooms occupied velvety forts of rotting stumps. Mica glistened; mud sloshed under boots; streams rushed down from mossy carpets above. A bobcat ambled by, saw us, and vanished into the dark forest. Down in the cove the gulf pounded the pebbly beach. We stretched out on the warm soil, listened to the rhythm of the sea, and tasted the sun in ripe berries.

Next morning we drove to the Atlantic side of the park, where the spectacular 185-mile-long Cabot Trail crosses the Aspy Fault. Here the earth's crust once had fractured and then moved like a giant seesaw: One side fell while the other rose. The pale morning sky was on fire. When we reached the beach we saw something thrashing in the surf. We ran. It was a beached whale, an immature pilot. Although only ten feet long, it probably weighed about 800 pounds. The surf kept pushing it farther up the beach.

We could not return it to the sea and felt utterly hopeless. The torpedo-shaped body, so graceful in water and so awkward on land, shivered as if the morning chill had penetrated its thick layer of blubber. Then the struggle was over. The whale was dead. We sat in the sand. My eyes were wet. John looked out to sea. "Do you think the mother is out there?" he asked. We fell silent again.

Nobody knows for sure why whales beach themselves. Maybe they are driven ashore by approaching death or disoriented by disturbances in their sonar system. The death of the pilot whale brought to mind the plight of all whales. The whaling industry in the North Atlantic flourished until the populations of blues, rights, and humpbacks were depleted. The Canadian government has now banned all commercial whaling; worldwide, the International Whaling Commission tries to regulate the harvest of whales, but its membership is voluntary.

The presence of whales in the Maritimes is linked to the abundant marine life in these waters. The abundance of fish and other marine organisms nourishes seabirds as well. Among nature's fishers, perhaps the most spectacular is the gannet. The largest gannetry in North America—with some 18,000 nesting pairs—is on Bonaventure Island, off the eastern shore of the Gaspé Peninsula.

"One almost feels sorry for the sea, they bombard it so fiercely," said John as we watched the gannets patrolling the water below the red cliffs of Bonaventure. From time to time a bird would fold back its three-foot-long wings and plunge in a steep dive. It would hit the water at about 60 miles an hour with a dull thud. Inflatable air sacs under its skin cushioned the impact.

The gannets, dazzling white birds with saffron heads, nest on ledges and on cliff tops, each pair just out of striking range of its neighbors. Gannets nest together, yet their aggressiveness and territoriality make them anything but peaceful bedfellows. As we watched, birds returning from the sea bit the napes of their mates; even mutual preening often turned into savage pecking.

Surf-furrowed boulders and worn pebbles record the signature of daily tides on Quebec's wild Gaspé Peninsula.

Gannets mate for life, and females, although strong and aggressive, instinctively turn their heads away from their mates in a gesture of appeasement. An all-out family fight would prevent the propagation of the species.

One bird stole a ball of moss and began to repair its sloppy nest. Another crash-landed and was attacked by its irate neighbors. Birds fed their dark-feathered offspring; agitated displays by individuals spread like waves across the colony. The continuous calls of "urrah-urrah" drowned out the noise of the sea below.

In recent years, the gannet breeding population on Bonaventure has decreased, and the hatching success here is only half that of other gannet colonies. The island became a provincial park in 1971, and the snowy birds are the main attraction. Unfortunately, tourist boats and visitors on foot often disturb the gannets. The birds also suffer from the same problems affecting most seabirds: Waterborne chemicals continue to impair their ability to reproduce, and fishing has reduced their food supply.

Stone-still, a furry marmot—also known as a woodchuck or a groundhog—ventures a cautious peek from its rocky perch on the Gaspé Peninsula's eastern shore.

Across the Bay of Gaspé from Bonaventure Island, a tilted wedge of land juts seaward between the bay and the mouth of the St. Lawrence River. This small peninsula of old Appalachian rocks, soaring cliffs, and underwater shelves that are a haven for scuba divers became Forillon National Park in 1970. We visited a seal colony in the park, east of Cap Bon Ami. The towering cliffs here resounded with the quarrels of tiny kittiwakes. Double-crested cormorants dried their wings, oblivious of the noise. In the chartreuse water around our boat, gray seals played the game of "now you see me, now you don't." A fat baby seal slept among the rocks, motionless until we came close; it dove with a succulent splash, accompanied by the raucous barking of adults.

When it rains in Forillon one can hole up with chief naturalist Maxime Saint-Amour, whose striking good looks make his family name all the more evocative. We talked with Max about the leading theme of the park, the harmony between man, the land, and the sea. "There is harmony in the surf eroding the rock of the cliff," said Max in his soft, French-tinted English. "We have to remember that this rock was born in the sea and that the sea will deposit its particles on the ocean floor, so they can become rock again.

"There is also harmony in the life of the black-backed gull, which preys on the eggs and young of other birds. Maybe its diet is not to our liking, but is it up to us to decide who should eat what?" And what of man's influence here? Forillon has magnificent prairies of wild flowers introduced by early settlers. The flowers now are part of the landscape: Man is always a part of his environment.

Rain persisted as we left Forillon and drove along the northeastern shore of Gaspé Peninsula. In the town of Ste.-Anne-des-Monts, near Gaspésian Provincial Park, we met a young park technician, Robert Picher. Robert, a restless wanderer, knows the park's Chic Chocs Mountains as intimately as anyone could hope to know hundreds of square miles of largely trackless country. We wanted to climb and to sleep on top of Mount Jacques Cartier, at 4,160 feet the highest peak in the region. Robert came along.

In the Chic Chocs the Appalachian chain was still with us. Here is a world of windswept mountaintops, bare rocks, racing clouds, and rivers that cascade from the heights. A large herd of woodland caribou, whose range is now restricted by the extensive logging in the valleys, shares this territory with moose and deer.

Robert had named the small hut on top of Mount Jacques Cartier "Chez Éole," for the Greek god of wind. The night there was appropriately windy, but peaceful. Next day John wrote: "We went this morning to look for caribou and, lo and behold, a caribou came to look at us. A young cow walked slowly downhill; Robert and I dropped down, hoping to look like rocks. It was the click of my camera that made her alert.

"She stepped downwind from us, her nostrils flared up and her body stiffened. I didn't move, and the caribou walked closer, her luminous eyes fixed on me, uncomprehending. I wondered if she would nudge me with her wet nose. Suddenly the wind billowed my parka, and she thundered down across the barrens."

ALL SUMMER WE HAD WANTED to run the Miramichi River, in New Brunswick. Yet every time we telephoned Bill Hooper, a provincial biologist who offered to take us there, he would say, "It's too low, we won't make it," or "It's too high and dangerous." Near the end of September the Miramichi was just right, but the weather was cold and wet. John stayed with Tara while I went to run the river.

Before the Europeans came, the Miramichi was one of the greatest Atlantic salmon spawning rivers. The first settlers in this region used tons of the fish as fertilizer. But by the time of the Canadian Confederation in 1867 there were few salmon left in most of the rivers. The Miramichi holds on as one of New Brunswick's last rivers with a large salmon run. But for how long? Pulp mills at the river's mouth, acid rain from the industrial regions to the west, and local spraying against spruce budworm all pollute the watershed.

One morning we put our canoes into the Miramichi near Half Moon Cove, in the upper, wilder part of the river. One 20-foot cedar canoe carried Bill Hooper and his wife, June. I climbed into another, carefully stepping over three long wooden poles, which Freddy Greene, a local ranger, had brought along. Standing in the stern, a poler must often hold the canoe back with all his might until it swings safely around rocks, which are too numerous to permit a quick run down the river with paddles. Freddy was busy with a pole, and I shivered in the cold drizzle.

"Don't you miss the summer?" I asked him.

"Yes," he replied. "All but the flies. The moose flies here are about the size of wasps and just as mean."

Autumn was upon us. Pale grasses swayed; red maple leaves raced along the gunwales; ducks took off with a loud whir of wings. "What do you look for as a fisherman?" I called to Bill as we emerged from the first set of rapids. "I look for pools with a long, fast current and rocks for fish to lie behind. See that big rock with small ones around it? We call that the Old Hen and Chickens Pool."

Dark and tall, Bill has a youthful quality. Years from now he will enter his old age kicking with energy. I asked Bill, "Spawning salmon don't feed in fresh water, so why do they rise to the fly?"

"They have just spent time feeding continuously in the sea," he said, "and their reflex now is to go after anything resembling food."

Born in the river, salmon descend to the sea after two or three years. One or two years later, they return to the river to spawn,

Hills ablaze with maple leaves brighten the shores of New Brunswick's Southwest Miramichi River. Once part of a prime logging area for the lofty white pines coveted by shipbuilders, the woods lining the banks of the Miramichi now thrive under the protection of private owners.

usually to the river of their birth. Superb athletes, they can jump waterfalls up to 12 feet high. No more than 10 percent of Atlantic salmon survive the ordeal of spawning. And, although one ten-pound salmon lays an average of 8,000 eggs, usually no more than two dozen of the fish that hatch live long enough to reproduce.

At our camp at Ranger Brook the men unloaded the canoes and went fishing. In the morning, falling snow settled on huge white pines, red maples, and the trembling gold of aspen and birch. While Bill fed curious Canadian jays, I looked at the map. "Bill, where are we? I see Little Southwest Miramichi, West Branch Little Southwest Miramichi, South Branch Northwest Miramichi—and even the Lower North Branch Little Southwest Miramichi."

"It's simple," said Bill. "You are on the Main Southwest Miramichi, just above Push-and-Be-Damned Rapids."

I asked Bill about the numerous camps we had seen along the river. "In New Brunswick a river can be privately owned, just like land," he told me. "Owners lease or sell the rights to fish and that's how we have all these camps for sportfishermen. Commercial fishing for Atlantic salmon was banned in New Brunswick from 1972 to 1980, after our stock was depleted. The government lifted the ban in 1981, although a quota is now enforced.

"I wish commercial fishing were still banned," Bill added, "especially offshore fishing, which has the greatest impact on our stock. Sportfishermen harvest far less than the amount caught by commercial fishermen, yet they contribute nearly ten times more to the economy."

As we set out again, the Miramichi meandered between high hills. We huddled in our canoes like ruffled birds. The river grew on me: A moose went crashing through the woods; the wind whistled; the rapids danced among the boulders. That night we feasted on mushrooms collected by June and on the last freshly caught salmon of the season. Next morning I recorded our run through the Burnt Hill rapids, the biggest that we faced.

"Here we come, river! It's bucking. It's jumping. Can Freddy avoid these boulders? Big breakers are bearing down on us. Hold the camera up, hold your breath, now! Ahhhh!"

Bill and June joined us below the rapids. "When we first ran the river, ten years ago, the federal wardens thought we would not survive," laughed June. "Not only had we an aluminum canoe, but I was a woman. In those days there were only guides and their sports." Yes, but what "sports." June once drank Scotch and water with Benny Goodman while on the Miramichi, and Freddy traveled here with Prince Charles.

The sun came out and threw a hue of copper on the river. Suddenly I remembered what Maxime Saint-Amour said on that rainy day in Forillon. "In wilderness," said Max, "we can get our equilibrium back just by watching water flow. Nature follows a reliable pattern. Season follows season. It's a faithful security that we cannot always count on in our relationships with other people, because they change, or they think differently than we do and we are surprised, maybe hurt. But nature does not surprise us in that sense."

The Miramichi flowed free. Come winter, it would be all ice and stillness. Then would come spring and new life. This certainty brought peace.

Gaspé tableaux: Tiered veil of water cascades at La Chute Waterfall on Cap-des-Rosiers Brook, in Quebec's Forillon National Park. Located at the northeastern tip of the Gaspé Peninsula, the park's rolling hills taper to a scarped finger of land. Sculpted by glaciers and the sea, cliffs of Forillon's Cap Bon Ami shelter a scalloped cove on the Gulf of St. Lawrence (opposite, lower). West of Forillon, the Gaspésian Provincial Park encompasses a vast plateau rumpled with peaks of the Chic Chocs Mountains (below)—home to deer, moose, and a herd of rare woodland caribou.

Wing-to-wing gannets crowd together on Bonaventure Island, a provincial park and bird sanctuary off the Gaspé Peninsula. A downy chick inserts its bill into its parent's to receive a partially digested meal of fish. Once slaughtered for their feathers and oil and for use as fish bait, gannets faded toward extinction at the turn of the century; in 1919 Canada set aside the Bonaventure refuge—with 36,000 breeding birds, now the largest gannetry in North America. Seaside wildlife flourishes along the Gaspé coast. On the Forillon Peninsula, two harbor seals bask along boulder-strewn shores (above). One curious people-watcher, a sleek gray seal, pops up for a closer look (opposite, top).

Autumn offers the ideal time for fishing the swift, cool waters of the Southwest Miramichi (above). Once ranked among the world's greatest Atlantic salmon spawning rivers, the Miramichi suffered a critical decline in populations during the 1960s, due to overfishing. An eight-year ban and the current strict quotas have begun to restore salmon stocks. Outfitters and clubs may lease portions of the Miramichi for sportfishing. On the last day of the season, provincial fisheries biologist Bill Hooper and his wife, June (right), cast for the big ones. Two salmon that rose to the fly (left) made a tasty dinner. After feeding in the sea, adult salmon return to rivers to spawn; the darker coloration of the fish on the left indicates it had been in fresh water longer than the fish at right. The Miramichi well represents the wilderness of Atlantic Canada: Though much of the land remains accessible to great numbers of people, just off the road, beyond the next ridge, the spirit of the wild endures.

The Canadian Shield

By Louis de la Haba · Photographs by Richard A. Cooke III

Smoothed by glaciers and the power of crashing waves, lichen-mottled bedrock of the Canadian Shield edges stormy Lake Superior in the wilderness of Pukaskwa National Park, in Ontario.

The Canadian Shield

THE STONE IN MY HAND seemed quite ordinary. It was oval in shape, and through it ran a thin vein of dull-white quartz. Patches of gray, black, and orange lichens clung to it, insinuating microscopic tendrils into invisible gaps in its smooth surface. It was the same tawny brown as the hills in the stark arctic landscape around me. As I looked at the stone, I tried to comprehend the immensity of time I could so easily enclose in my fist, for this fragment of the austere scene was part of the Canadian Shield, an expanse of bedrock dating from Precambrian times—the period between the formation of the earth, estimated by geologists at about four billion, six hundred million years ago, and the next geologic era, the Paleozoic, about six hundred million years ago. The little stone, then, was the very stuff of which the continents were formed, though not the continents as we know them. It came from a point somewhere in the abyss of time when the earth was still young, and the first appearance of life was still many millions of years in the future.

Precambrian rock, everywhere else buried beneath thousands of feet of younger deposits, appears on or near the surface of portions of every continent. But nowhere is it as extensive, as integral a part of the topography, as in Canada. The Canadian Shield—so-called because of its saucer, or shield, shape when viewed in cross section—covers about half the country, an incredible 1,771,000 square miles. Precambrian rock extends into the Canadian Arctic Archipelago and into Greenland, but its mass lies on the mainland, where its outer edge sweeps in a huge arc from northern Labrador south to the St. Lawrence River, westward through the Great Lakes, then northwest again to the arctic seas. The Shield does not stop at the Canadian-U. S. border, but reaches into parts of Minnesota, Wisconsin, and Michigan, and into the forested Adirondack Mountains of New York State.

The Shield is not all of a piece, containing many varieties of rock of diverse ages. Everywhere it has been flattened, broken, pushed, gouged, and scoured by glaciers from several ice ages. This has left a confused surface drainage with some well-defined rivers, thousands of lakes and ponds—far too many to have individual names—and spongy muskeg. In the north, beyond the tree line, the Shield forms Canada's Barren Grounds, an enormous area of rolling, rocky tundra, underlain by permafrost. It is a place where plants seldom grow taller than a few inches, where temperatures regularly drop to 40 below zero, and where unhindered winds can turn this into a windchill factor of more than 100 below.

On the edge of the tundra, the tree line traces an arc that faintly echoes the sweep of the Shield. In this transitional zone, winds and temperatures are not so fiercely inhospitable, and small accumulations of soil lend precarious footing to sparsely growing trees. Beyond this zone, trees grow taller and closer together, and grade into the spruce-birch-aspen boreal forest that is so much a part of the image of the Canadian wilderness.

I was to spend more than two months in the Canadian Shield country, constantly aware of its raw beauty and ever reminded of its harsh, unforgiving power. In the northern barrens where I now stood, everything was bedrock, muskeg, and water, water, water. This is home to the barren-ground grizzly and the polar bear, to the tundra wolf, the musk-ox, the fox, and the lemming. Snowy owls,

ARCTIC OCEAN

GREENLAND
(Denmark)

*eaufort
Sea*

*Great
Bear
Lake*

NORTHWEST TERRITORIES

*Bathurst
Inlet*

Hood ●Umingmaktok
●**Bathurst Inlet**
Burnside River

ARCTIC CIRCLE

THELON GAME
SANCTUARY

★Yellowknife ●**Baker Lake**
●Reliance

Thelon

Great Slave Lake

Rankin Inlet● ●**Chesterfield
Inlet**

Tree Line

BERTA

*Lake
Athabasca*

*Reindeer
Lake*

Churchill

Lynn
Lake

●Churchill

*Labrador
Sea*

*Ungava
Bay*

Fort Chimo●

George

Tree Line

Labrador

Hudson Bay

Schefferville●

NEWFOUNDLAND

MANITOBA

SASKATCH-
EWAN

Regina ★

Berens

*Lake
Winnipeg* ●Little
Grand
Rapids

ONTARIO

*James
Bay*

QUEBEC

CANADA
UNITED STATES

Winnipeg ★

PUKASKWA
NATIONAL
PARK

LA MAURICIE
NATIONAL PARK

CAP TOURMENTE
NATIONAL
WILDLIFE AREA

MONT TREMBLANT
PROVINCIAL PARK

St. Lawrence

Lake Superior

Sault Ste. Marie●

Quebec

Ottawa ★

●Montreal

*Lake
Huron*

*Lake
Michigan*

Toronto ★

Lake Ontario

Lake Erie

*Within the vast Canadian
Shield—an area covering
nearly half of Canada—lies an
expanse of bedrock containing some
of the oldest rocks on earth. The
broad arc of the Shield sweeps from
northern Labrador to the Great Lakes
and northwest to the arctic coast, encompassing
a land of sharp contrasts. Dense boreal forests
in the south gradually thin out, yielding beyond the
tree line to the tundra of the Barren Grounds—a bleak country
where muskeg, rock, and water spread in seemingly endless
undulations. Except for petroleum and natural gas, the Shield
holds a major part of Canada's mineral wealth, much of it as yet
untapped. This forbidding region remains largely uninhabited:
Only about 10 percent of Canada's population lives on the Shield.*

ATLANTIC
OCEAN

0   KILOMETERS   500

0   STATUTE MILES   500

ptarmigans, and ravens live here the year long; swans and geese, eagles, hawks, and falcons, among scores of other avian species, come to nest in spring and summer. This vast and empty land is also home to the Inuit, and to a relatively small but slowly growing handful of *kabloonas*, white persons.

I put my thought-provoking little stone in my pocket and walked on, stepping on a carpet of similar stones that crunched beneath my boots. I had been following a windswept ridge above Bathurst Inlet, an arm of Coronation Gulf in Canada's Northwest Territories. The ground around me was empty of vegetation, save for fragile tufts of white mountain avens, yellow cinquefoils, and the purple of occasional rhododendrons that grew only three or four inches high. The flowers bloomed on protected slopes below the ridge and at the base of sheltering boulders in an explosion of life and color that is one of the visual rewards of the arctic spring, when every plant, in a frenzy of growth, struggles to capture the sun's beneficent energy.

The day was June 26, only five days after the summer solstice and the arrival of the midnight sun in these latitudes. The air was comfortably warm. The sky was free of clouds, pellucid, overwhelming in its luminous intensity. Below me, on both sides, spread the steely blue of arctic waters—a lake to the right, another to the left, one flowing into the other through a shadowed ravine and a tumultuous waterfall. Beyond, to my left, last winter's ice was beginning to break up in the inlet, and out of it rose the barren tops of islands. On a hillock a half-mile or more away, my tent stood near the shore of Fishing Lake, a speck of color against the monochrome ground.

Before coming here, I had been staying at the Bathurst Inlet Lodge, at the mouth of the Burnside River. The lodge is an old Hudson's Bay Company post where many Inuit formerly came to trade furs for such items as guns, ammunition, tea, tobacco, and flour. Until it closed in 1964, as many as a hundred Inuit families would gather around the post at trading time and build their snowhouses there. Roman Catholic missionaries lived at Bathurst then, and their red-roofed, steepled chapel is now part of the lodge accommodations. Now only about two dozen Inuit live at Bathurst Inlet the year round.

Choosing to camp out for a better feel of the country, I had taken a long, cold boat ride to Fishing Lake, a small arm of Bathurst Inlet. My guide was Henry Kamaoyok, a local Inuit who speaks a stumbling English that often as not turns into irrepressible laughter. Henry is a remarkable fellow, a good hunter I was told, though he walks with a limp because of polio contracted in his youth.

After we landed on a narrow beach, Henry led the way past a growth of dwarf willows to a flat spot at the top of a knoll. Ground squirrels—called sik-sik—had dug their burrows here, and in places the ground had been torn up by the powerful claws of a grizzly looking for a meal. Henry suggested I set up my tent here.

Nearby I saw several oblong arrangements of rocks such as the Inuit use to hold down their tents. Fragments of caribou bones lay strewn about, and Henry said this was one of the places where he and his relatives camped when hunting and fishing. As I unfolded my tent, Henry watched with interest and asked me about it.

Would it stand up to the wind? Would it keep out mosquitoes? Was it very expensive? "First class," Henry said as I gave my answers. "First class." It was a phrase he had heard me use the day before.

Henry stayed for the mandatory cup of tea, then I walked with him to the boat. Someone would come for me in a day or so. On the little beach, Henry stooped to peer at the tracks of a wolf and two bears. "Big bear," he said, "and her little one." The larger bear's tracks seemed enormous to me. Five clearly defined holes in the sand, imprinted by the animal's claws, extended fully four inches beyond the rounded depressions left by the toe pads.

Henry looked at me and laughed. He must have read my mind—I had been worrying that my tent wasn't more than 50 yards from the grizzly bear promenade. Then he got into the boat, started the motor, and called out, "Don't let the bears eat you!"

I went for a long hike, returning in broad daylight around 10 p.m. After supper, I crawled into my tent and sleeping bag and closed my eyes in the unaccustomed light. I was almost asleep when I heard a sound, as of an animal panting. I was out of bag and tent in record time, thinking a wolf might be prowling outside, but there was nothing. Then I heard the sound again and looked up in time to see a raven flying over. The panting was the sound of its wings beating the air. It was the only sound in the stillness of the arctic night.

On the way in with Henry, I had seen a small herd of musk-oxen grazing in a valley nearby. Next morning I went off in search of them. The footing was treacherous on hummocks of sedge that rolled under my feet. I had to cross a low spot wet with melting snow and push my way through a willow thicket where I found tufts of qiviut, the winter wool undercoat that musk-oxen shed in spring. Inuit women used to gather this wonderfully light and warm wool to make clothing. Now, with factory-made materials easily available, it is something of a rarity to find an article made of qiviut. Trish Warner, who owns the lodge at Bathurst with her husband, Glenn, had shown me a scarf she had—it was almost a yard long and five or six inches wide, fluffy, and nearly weightless.

Climbing a hillside, I peered over the top of a ridge and saw four musk-oxen in the narrow valley below. It was a scene out of the Ice Age. Musk-oxen are survivors of the Pleistocene epoch—a time that witnessed the extinction of most large northern mammals. The great beasts were shaggy and massive, with enormous black eyes, shiny, wet noses, and solid, downturned horns.

They grazed unconcerned on the sedge, moving slowly along the damp valley floor. After a while, the biggest of the bulls lay down to chew his cud, forelegs stretched straight to the front the way a dog will sometimes lie. The others moved a short distance away and soon began a fascinating game in which two of them would back away, face each other, then come galloping full tilt to meet with a great, jarring crash. The fourth one, the big bull, by now was lying on his side, dozing in the sun.

The rutting season for musk-oxen begins in late July. Bulls fight each other for dominance. The winners get the cows. The young bulls I was watching were rehearsing for the approaching events, but I thought they would have to wait a few more years. They were no match for the big bull that lay at rest.

Stark uplands rise abruptly from the steely waters of Bathurst Inlet, in Canada's Northwest Territories. Here in the northern Shield, muskoxen roam in peaceful isolation, and migratory birds come to nest around the many lakes and in rockbound aeries. On the western shore of Bathurst Inlet, a nature lodge for summer visitors occupies a former trading post, and a few Inuit families pursue their traditional life-style.

On my last day at Fishing Lake, I examined the area where the grizzly had been digging into the sik-sik mound. Exposed on the thin, grayish brown soil I found a scattering of stone flakes and chips and a couple of broken stone points—the tips of spears, perhaps, or arrows. I recognized this as what archaeologists call a workshop, a place where someone long ago had sat making tools out of stone. The debris was the by-product of the toolmaker's work as he shaped his artifacts. The broken points, most likely, were simple mistakes he had left lying on the ground.

Glenn Warner told me later that archaeologists had excavated a similar site on another hill nearby and determined that it had been occupied more than 2,000 years ago. So hunters had come here then. It seemed quite logical. Both sites—the one so neatly uncovered by the bear and the one the archaeologists had excavated—were ideal for hunters. Both commanded a wide view, so people could see any animals that moved in the area. Both were fairly well protected from the wind by ridges, and both were close to the lake. It was no surprise, either, that Henry and his people also came here to hunt and fish. It had been a good place for that for centuries.

ON MY RETURN TO THE LODGE, I visited the Inuit community. The Bathurst Inlet Inuit still hunt, fish, and trap much as they always have. A few keep dogs to pull their sleds, though most have snowmobiles—skidoos, as they are called throughout the north. In the summer, when the lodge is open, the men work as nature and fishing guides and do chores around the lodge. The women provide kitchen and housekeeping help.

Though the Bathurst Inuit lead fairly traditional lives, most of Canada's estimated 17,550 Inuit live in settlements. Many families have abandoned the isolated hunting camps in which they once lived for places such as Chesterfield Inlet, Rankin Inlet, and Baker Lake, where there are airfields, medical and welfare agencies, police, cooperatives that sell soapstone carvings and other Inuit arts and crafts, and the inevitable Hudson's Bay Company store—"The Bay," usually the only store in town.

The Hudson's Bay store at Bathurst Inlet was established in

1930. Before it opened, no permanent settlement existed. The Inuit came and went with the seasons, living in snowhouses or in tents made of caribou hide. One day in 1912, two white men showed up at Bathurst: Harry V. Radford, an American, and a young Canadian named T. G. Street. The two men got into a fight with a group of Inuit and were killed, thereby launching a patrol by Canada's Mounted Police that ranks as one of the most famous in the annals of the force, even though, that time, the police didn't "get their man."

Word of the slayings took some time to reach the authorities in the south. In 1914, one patrol set out from Halifax, Nova Scotia, to investigate but had to turn back because of bad weather. Not until 1917 were the Mounted Police able to reach Bathurst Inlet. In the spring, Inspector F. H. French and Sgt. Maj. T. B. Caulkin left Baker Lake for Bathurst and were soon beset by "wretched conditions," as French wrote in his report. Blizzards forced them to hole up repeatedly, and the barren, rugged terrain caused long detours. Food supplies dwindled with each passing week, and the threat of starvation loomed ever larger. French and Caulkin did not arrive at Bathurst Inlet until almost two months after they had left Baker Lake.

At Bathurst, they found that the alleged killers had vanished. Witnesses to the fatal incident told the police that Radford had physically abused one of two guides he and Street had hired. Three other Inuit came to the guide's assistance and, in the ensuing fight, the two white men were speared. "From the statements inclosed and from the conversations I had with different natives along the coast," French reported, "I would judge that [the Inuit] only acted in self-defence and to protect themselves. . . ."

For French and Caulkin, the way back to Baker Lake was even more difficult than the trip to Bathurst. Heavy snows, lashing winds, and fog slowed them down, but they slogged on until they reached their detachment. French had kept track of the miles traveled, including distances covered while hunting and while searching for Inuit encampments. The total came to 5,153 miles; the time spent on patrol: from March 21, 1917, to January 29, 1918.

On their return journey, French and Caulkin had struggled through a wild portion of the Barren Grounds that, in 1927, was set aside by the Canadian government as the Thelon Game Sanctuary. An uninhabited, 21,500-square-mile area, the sanctuary encompasses the lower waters of the Hanbury and the Clarke, all of the Finnie and the Tammarvi Rivers, as well as much of the Thelon itself, which flows generally east through the tundra to its outlet into Baker Lake.

The valleys of the Thelon and its tributaries, though far beyond the tree line, provide sufficient shelter from arctic winds to allow for sizable growths of spruce and scrub willow. The valleys constitute, in effect, a green oasis in the northern desert of gray rocks and lichens. Sandy eskers, deposits left by ancient rivers that once flowed under the ice sheet that covered the north, snake across the countryside. Eskers consist of loosely compacted sand, gravel, and river boulders. In places near existing rivers, where the sand forms dunes and valleys, spruce trees grow in a parklike setting.

In Yellowknife, a town of about 9,500 that is the capital of the Northwest Territories, I met Robert J. Decker, a biologist with the territorial wildlife service. Bob is a native *(Continued on page 66)*

Savoring a northern delicacy, John Akana, an Inuk from the community of Umingmaktok, on the northeastern shore of Bathurst Inlet, scrapes marrow from a caribou leg bone. The Inuit prize marrow because of its high content of fat, an energy-giving essential in the Arctic. Bathurst Inlet's Inuit have declined government offers to move them to more modern settlements, preferring to retain their independence as hunters and fishermen.

*Day's harvest of silvery char dries under a pallid summer sun
at a fishing camp along Bathurst Inlet's shoreline. During the mild
summers in this area, many Inuit range far from their winter homes
on hunting and fishing expeditions. A widow, Mrs. Jessie Hakungak
(above, at left), and her two children, Lorraine and Colin, traveled here
from their village with John Akana, Mrs. Hakungak's brother-in-law.
At left, Colin scoops smelt caught with a net onto the shore, where
his sister and mother will help gather them. Split, boned, and dried,
the fish will provide food during the winter months.*

Seething with foam, the Hood River plunges through a rocky maze at Wilberforce Falls. The roaring

160-foot cataract near Bathurst Inlet ranks as the highest in Canada north of the Arctic Circle.

Abloom in the northern spring, clusters of moss campion cloak a hillside with patches of lavender. During the short summer growing season, masses of color splash the Barren Grounds. Most plants grow no higher than a few inches. Close to the ground, they can efficiently capture the sun's warming rays and find shelter from cold, blustery winds.

of the north, and his job requires him to travel widely, keeping track of wildlife populations. He knows the Thelon well and has canoed the Clarke. Bob told me that the sanctuary was established at a time when the musk-ox population had decreased dangerously due to overhunting. "In the arctic islands," Bob said, "early explorers had been shooting the animals for years for meat. And when the bison were just about eliminated on the Great Plains because of the demand for hides for carriage robes, the musk-oxen on the mainland were hit really hard. The Hudson's Bay Company was paying good money for the hides, so local hunters went after the musk-oxen."

"Musk-oxen are doing extremely well now throughout much of their range. But even when the herds had decreased drastically, the Thelon was noted for musk-oxen because the area was so inaccessible that they weren't hunted there. There were musk-oxen around the Thelon when John Hornby went through in the 1920s."

John Hornby is a favorite subject of Bob's. Hornby was an Englishman who came to Canada in 1904 and fell in love with the trackless, solitary north. For years he knocked about the country, often alone. Canadian maps bear witness to his ubiquitous presence: Hornby Bay, Hornby Hill, Hornby Creek, Hornby Channel, and on the Thelon River, near his grave, Hornby Point.

In 1925, accompanied by a fellow Englishman, Hornby traveled from Great Slave Lake to Chesterfield Inlet on a government commission to report on the wildlife of the Thelon River area. Hornby recommended establishment of a game sanctuary for the preservation of musk-oxen, and his report contributed to the government's decision to do so a short time later.

Hornby had been much impressed by the Thelon, and he especially remembered an inviting grove of spruce trees near a bend in the river. Late in 1925 he had to return to England, where his father was dying. While there, he met Edgar Christian, 17-year-old son of his first cousin Marguerite Hornby Christian. The young man was mesmerized by Hornby's stories of the distant wilderness. When Hornby returned to Canada, Edgar went with him with the blessing of his father, Col. Wilfred F. Christian, who thought the experience would give the youth something to build his life on.

Edgar and Hornby traveled to Edmonton, Alberta, to make preparations for a trip to the Thelon. Hornby hoped to build a cabin in the spruce grove he so vividly remembered, to spend the winter reaping a rich harvest of furs, and then to make his way to Chesterfield Inlet in time to catch an outgoing Hudson's Bay Company schooner. In Edmonton, Hornby and Edgar were joined by Harold Adlard, another young immigrant from England. By June 10, 1926, the three were on Great Slave Lake with equipment that included a large canoe and a heavy load of supplies, among which was—as Edgar wrote his father—"some grub to Last till the winter comes & then we kill meat which will keep in the snow & ice."

Hornby and his companions began their journey late in the year and dawdled along the way. A note Hornby left in a metal canister at Deville Lake read: "About Aug. 5th 1926. Owing to bad weather and laziness, travelling slowly. One big migration of caribou passed. . . ." Fateful words. By the time the party reached the Thelon, the caribou herds they had been relying on for meat had all moved south.

Edgar Christian kept a diary. His first entry from the spruce grove was dated October 14. The men were living in tents while building a small log cabin. It was not long before their sufferings began. There were no caribou; they saw no musk-oxen. They caught few animals in their traps—an occasional hare, some foxes, the odd wolverine. (The taste of wolverine has been compared to that of skunk.) They caught some fish in nets they had laboriously strung in the frozen Thelon. They shot ptarmigan or, once in a while, caught them in nets.

The men ate all these animals, then boiled the bones and drank the thin broth, and then they boiled the offal they had thrown away and ate that. Hornby and Adlard went out repeatedly to hunt, most often returning home empty-handed. The intense cold, wind, and snow weakened them as winter wore on. On April 16, 1927, Hornby died. He had been secretly starving himself so the others would have more to eat. Edgar and Adlard wrapped his body in canvas and burlap and placed it outside the cabin door. Adlard died on May 3, and Edgar was left alone, grubbing for food. Thus Edgar lingered, slowly starving. Early in June, he wrote his mother and father and placed his letters and diary in the cold stove. On it he left a note: "WHO [illegible] LOOK IN STOVE." Then he crawled into his bunk under his Hudson's Bay blankets to die.

The three bodies were discovered more than a year later by a party that had been canoeing down the Thelon. But the Mounted Police did not reach the cabin until July 25, 1929—more than two years after Edgar had died. They buried Hornby and his companions near the cabin and marked the graves with wooden crosses.

BOB DECKER TOLD ME THE STORY of John Hornby over lunch one day and said he had a friend I might like to meet, someone who lives on the Thelon. A few days later, he introduced me to Roger Catling, a blond, lithely built man in his late 20s. Roger is a professional wolf hunter. In summer, he lives in the tiny community of Reliance with his Chipewyan Indian wife, Theresa, and their two daughters. In winter, the family moves to a cabin Roger built on the Thelon, outside the sanctuary, and he and Theresa go hunting and trapping.

Roger makes a good living. Wolves are plentiful in this area; in the view of many, excessively so. The work is demanding. A typical day begins at daybreak. Roger leaves the cabin on his skidoo and hunts until dark in the bitter cold. Prices for pelts are good, averaging around $475 Canadian, but Roger has been paid as much as $700 for a single skin at the fur auction in Edmonton. He hunts caribou for fresh meat and also traps for foxes and wolverines.

Roger owns a Super Cub, a single-engine aircraft equipped with floats that, in winter, he replaces with skis. I arranged to spend a week on the Thelon with him, and we flew out of Yellowknife one morning. By midafternoon we were on the upper reaches of the river, where it flows through a lake in front of Roger's cabin. All around the cabin, on the ground, lay wide sheets of plywood with hundreds of nails hammered through them, pointed ends up. "To keep out grizzlies," he explained.

"One time when we weren't here, a bear tore the house all to pieces. It opened 150 to 200 cans of food, spilled and ate sugar and flour, and broke all the windows." Roger and Theresa have also had

Its exposed roots seeking a firm anchor, a gnarled hardwood clings to a moss-covered outcropping at Mont Tremblant Provincial Park, in southern Quebec. Even in forested areas, the Shield rock lies so close to the surface that trees must develop wide-spreading root systems to survive.

several face-to-face encounters with grizzlies. Outside the cabin, Roger never goes without his powerful .44-magnum revolver.

Next morning we took off for the sanctuary, flying over a portion of the Hanbury River and its many falls and rapids. It was hard for me to imagine how Hornby could have negotiated the difficult portages around the swift waters and rocky canyons. We flew over several camps from which geologists were exploring the tundra for minerals. The Shield is too old geologically to have fossil fuels. But it is full of valuable minerals—and of people looking for them. German, British, French, American, and Canadian firms are all busy with exploration. So far, there has been no extensive mining activity on the Barren Grounds, but many people are concerned about the effect on the tundra's ecological balance when the moment comes.

Entombed in the Shield's ancient bedrock is a wealth of gold, silver, lead, nickel, zinc, iron, copper, and asbestos. And there is uranium. A good deal of the exploration is for uranium-bearing rock. The cost of this work is phenomenal. Aircraft provide the only transport for people and supplies, and for the exploration work as well. A gallon of aircraft fuel delivered to the Barren Grounds costs about $10; a large helicopter can guzzle that in a minute.

As the tundra unfolded beneath us, I looked at the many lakes. On the Shield, there is about as much water as land. I saw lakes with islands in them, and lakes with islands that had their own little lakes. Their shapes were infinitely varied, like those of clouds. One lake Roger pointed out bears the name of Cosmos. This was where a Canadian-U. S. military and scientific team spent part of a winter recovering fragments of a Soviet nuclear-powered satellite—*Cosmos 954*—which crashed in Canada on January 24, 1978.

Flying over the Thelon and its wooded banks, we saw moose and musk-oxen and Canada geese that were unable to fly because they were in molt. Over the intercom, Roger told me to look down to our left. A large male grizzly bear was moving through the willows, glistening in the sun, his fur almost blond. I could see his powerful shoulder and haunch muscles rippling under thick layers of fat and fur. Roger lowered the wing flaps to slow us down. The grizzly is lord of the barrens and has no fear. As we approached the bear below, he stood up and sniffed nearsightedly in our direction. Then, as we passed over him, he swiped at us with an enormous outspread paw. I cringed involuntarily, even though we were at least a hundred feet above him.

We landed on the Thelon, not far from where the bear had been but on the opposite bank, and pushed our way through the willows and into the spruce trees. There we found the remains of John Hornby's cabin. The roof had caved in long before, but parts of the walls were still standing. With his hunter's outlook, Roger thought it was a terrible place for a cabin. "Even if the caribou walked right in front of it along the river, you'd never see them. The trees are too thick," he said.

A few steps from the cabin were the graves. The initials the Mounted Police had carved on the crosses were still legible. "E. C.," "J. H.," "H. A." Bits of moss and lichen grew on the weathered wood. In silence, we left to set up camp near Hornby Point, a short distance away, on a rocky bank above a cobble beach.

Here on the Thelon I experienced full force the "scourges of the

north"—mosquitoes and tiny black flies. There had been mosquitoes at Bathurst Inlet and in other places I had visited, but nothing like the numbers I encountered on the Thelon. Mosquitoes and black flies breed by the billion in the many lakes and streams on the Shield. At times they are so numerous they can drive animals insane. They can clog the nostrils of moose and caribou. The late Dr. Bryan Hocking, of the University of Alberta, reported that under attack by black flies, "a susceptible person can become worked up into an emotional state bordering on dementia."

At Hornby Point the insects were swarming. We decided not to cook that night—all we'd get would be mosquito stew. Later, in the tent, I could hear the insects' wings and feet brushing against the nylon. It sounded exactly like gently falling rain. The insects were to plague us throughout our stay on the Thelon.

MOSQUITOES AND FLIES in large concentrations may affect the migration routes of the caribou, an animal that many inhabitants of the Shield depend on for food. Three major caribou herds are found on the portion of the Shield that lies within the mainland Northwest Territories—the Bathurst herd in the western Shield, the Beverly herd in the area of the Thelon, and the Kaminuriak herd in the east. A fourth great herd, the George River, roams through northern Quebec and Labrador. The Bathurst, Beverly, and Kaminuriak herds migrate north in the spring to calve. The animals stay in the north for the summer; in the fall, they return south, sometimes going into Saskatchewan, Manitoba, and western Ontario.

The caribou follow routes they have used since time immemorial. But when insects, weather, or forest fires cause changes in the routes, and the herds fail to show up at the expected places, the impact on the local people can be devastating.

Despite their great numbers, in the immensity of the north the caribou can disappear with almost magical effect. They are restless animals, almost always on the move. I was in Yellowknife one day when Dr. Anne Gunn, a biologist with the Northwest Territories Wildlife Service, received news that a herd of 10,000 to 12,000 animals had been observed milling around the area of Sand Lake.

Eager to see a large aggregation of (Continued on page 78)

Desolate Chesterfield Inlet evokes the words of an 18th-century traveler on the Barren Grounds: "A deathly stillness hangs over all and the oppressive loneliness weighs upon the spectator...." Today some 250 people, mostly Inuit and a few whites, live in an isolated outpost near where Chesterfield Inlet joins Hudson Bay.

Her thick fur golden in the sun, a mother grizzly moves to protect her cub in the Thelon Game Sanctuary, swiping an outstretched paw at a passing airplane. The 21,500-square-mile sanctuary, whose wooded banks trace a band of green across the treeless tundra, lies within the Barren Grounds. Established in 1927 primarily as a haven for musk-oxen, the refuge harbors a wide variety of other wildlife as well, including bears, moose, caribou, wolves, foxes, and migratory birds. Wings flapping and webbed feet churning, a flock of Canada geese (below) skims the waters of the Thelon River.

Wooded oasis on the barren tundra, an esker (right) winds its sinuous way near Howard Lake. Below, another esker forms a sandy stretch of shoreline along the nearby Thelon River. Once the beds of rivers that flowed under melting ice sheets some 9,000 years ago, eskers now raise their sand and gravel ridges above the tundra's generally flat terrain. Uncounted lakes of every conceivable shape and size paint the land with sky-reflected blue. Eskers provide shelter from winter storms, permitting small groves of spruce to grow well beyond the tree line. Wolves and foxes dig their dens in the sand among the roots of trees, and caribou often travel along the eskers, leaving their trails—visible at right—on the ridgetops. The wooded country of the Thelon increasingly attracts moose, which have ranged there from their usual forest habitat.

Ghostly mists enshroud skeletal tree trunks at Reindeer Lake. A dam built in 1942 on

the Reindeer River raised the level of the lake, drowning part of the surrounding forest.

Dense boreal growth rims the rocky shoreline of Reindeer Lake, on the border of Saskatchewan and Manitoba. A wealth of furbearing animals—foxes, lynxes, otters, beavers, and bears—brought European trappers to the vast wilderness of the boreal forest. At Reindeer Lake, many of the local Cree Indians still set traplines in winter. Today prospectors probe the ancient rocks for minerals, and the lake's cold, clear waters support an extensive fishing industry. At right, a black bear emerges from the forest near the lake. In spring bears prowl the shore in search of fish that enter shallow streams to spawn.

caribou, I flew to Baker Lake, landing amid thickening fog. For four days I was fogbound, unable to fly. On the fifth day the fog lifted, and I left for Sand Lake in an aging single-engine Beaver. Although the pilot flew in widening circles for nearly six hours, I didn't see a single caribou. Pressed by their migratory urge, they had moved on.

The main predator of the caribou is man. Wolves, which follow the herds in their migrations, also make many kills, especially on the calving grounds, where the caribou are most vulnerable. Bears, foxes, wolverines, and ravens all feed on carcasses left by wolves, so that the caribou justifies its reputation as the lifeline of the north. "Caribou are the mainstay of the country," I remembered Roger Catling saying. "If they weren't here, we wouldn't be here." But because of the pressures of hunting and animal predation, the barren-ground caribou are in trouble. Biologists estimate

Perched on a flower-sprinkled ledge, a tundra peregrine falcon warily guards its aerie. The swift predators range well into South America but nest in remote reaches of the tundra. Peregrines, an endangered species, prey on other birds in flight. On hunting dives, with wings half folded, they can plummet toward their quarry at speeds of up to 175 miles an hour.

In a froth of white water, the Berens River (opposite) cascades at Little Grand Rapids, in southeastern Manitoba. Part of the Shield's interior drainage, the Berens flows into Lake Winnipeg, third largest Canadian lake, after Great Bear and Great Slave.

that at one time there may have been two to three million caribou on the Barren Grounds. Estimates made in 1981 placed the number at about 400,000.

Native hunters may legally kill as many caribou as they wish. There are no quotas because the Canadian government is loath to interfere with traditional native rights. Hardest hit of the herds is the Kaminuriak, whose migrations bring it close to population centers. The Kaminuriak herd once numbered more than 100,000. By 1980 it had declined to 38,000. A widely circulated wildlife service poster warns that if present rates of hunting and predation continue, "the herd will probably decrease to less than 10,000 animals in the next 10 years."

Dr. Cormack Gates, a wildlife service biologist at Rankin Inlet, estimated the 1980 kill to be about 4,500—more than 10 percent of the population. The high mobility afforded hunters by skidoos, and the widespread use of repeating rifles, are inflicting losses the herds cannot absorb, he told me. When I asked whether the Inuit were aware of this, he suggested I talk with a local hunter. With an interpreter, I went to an Inuit camp a few miles from Rankin and met an old hunter named John Makkigak. I mentioned the declining caribou population, and he responded vehemently: "I don't believe that. They [the biologists] don't know how to count caribou."

I remembered my talk with Dr. Gunn. She had spoken of the "credibility problem" with the native people. "It's hard to convince them that the animals are declining. It's difficult to believe caribou are on the decline when you're standing in the middle of a herd of thousands. It's only when you look at the larger area that you see there are fewer caribou."

One major Shield herd is, surprisingly, growing in numbers—the George River herd, in northern Quebec and Labrador. Biologist Ian Juniper of the Quebec Department of Recreation, Fish, and Game told me that the herd had grown from 178,000 animals in 1976 to an astounding 374,000 in the fall of 1981—all estimates, of course. "I think it's safe to say that this is the largest herd of wild caribou in the world. And they're not heavily hunted, either by native people or by sport hunters," Ian said.

To see the herd, I traveled with Ian to the town of Schefferville, in northern Quebec, and from there flew over the George River area. It was autumn, and the caribou were beginning to gather for the fall migration and the annual rut. The landscape was streaked with the gold of tamarack trees growing in bands and clusters among the darker spruce. The Shield here has been deeply scoured by ice age glaciers, and there are many lakes cradled in straight, rocky, V-shaped valleys that stretch blue fingers to the horizon.

The weather in northern Quebec had been unseasonably warm. We had expected to find the caribou already massed for migration, or perhaps already on the move, but because of the warmth, they were still milling aimlessly in loose, scattered groups. In all, we saw only a few thousand animals spread over a fairly wide area. But the sight was impressive nevertheless, for the caribou were in prime condition. "See how fat they are and how beautiful their coats and antlers look," Ian said. "They're at their best at this time of year."

NORTHERN QUEBEC was the last place I visited in the tundra of the northern Shield. Earlier, I had spent some time in Churchill, Manitoba, a port on Hudson Bay, to see the tundra-forest transition zone. The first time I went there, late in June, the bay was solidly frozen. The polar bears for which Churchill is famous were still out on the ice, hunting for seals. Hudson Bay is so large that it creates its own weather, and though the Churchill area is far south of the Arctic Circle, under the bay's influence its environment is partly arctic.

Three distinct environments come together at Churchill: the maritime Hudson Bay shoreline, the tundra, and the boreal forest. There are many bogs and ponds in the area and stunted arctic plants like the ones I had seen at Bathurst Inlet. But trees also grow here. The willows are thick along streams and ponds. Spruces grow here, too—in some places, more or less solitary; in others, clustered in extensive groupings that presage the boreal forest farther south and west. In spring, migratory birds funnel through the Churchill area in the hundreds of thousands, some to nest here, others on their way to nesting grounds farther north.

Once you enter the boreal forest, which stretches to the rim of the Shield, the contrast with the tundra is overwhelming. In the forest, or taiga, the Shield rock appears in lichen- and moss-covered outcroppings. But the trees make an almost impenetrable cover. Toward the periphery of the Shield grow mixed forests of birch, aspen, pine, balsam fir, hemlock, and the predominant white spruce and black spruce. One biologist has referred to the boreal forest as

Watchful mother and her cubs forage along the shore of Hudson Bay, near Churchill, Manitoba. Swift and powerful, polar bears rule the north. In winter they live on the sea ice, enduring the harshest of conditions in their endless quest for seals. With the summer breakup of the ice, they come ashore. Because many polar bears den south of Churchill, the town calls itself the "polar bear capital of the world."

the "spruce-moose" forest. Moose are abundant, as are woodland caribou. Black bears, wolves, wolverines, foxes, lynxes, otters, martens, minks, beavers, and other furbearers are plentiful. This is the country early explorers of Canada traveled through and where trappers and voyageurs tapped the wilderness for its seemingly inexhaustible supply of furs for the upper classes of Europe.

To preserve a portion of the boreal forest, the Canadian government has set aside the 725-square-mile Pukaskwa National Park, on the northeast shore of Lake Superior. The park is a paradise for hikers and canoeists. A 40-mile-long wilderness trail follows the shoreline, crossing sandy beaches and wooded cliff tops where the massive rock of the Canadian Shield plunges into the lake, and at times cutting inland through the dense, fragrant forest.

I went to Pukaskwa in the autumn and found it virtually empty of visitors. A storm was brewing on Superior—the legendary "Gitche Gumee" of the poet Longfellow. Superior is a body of water about which Chief Park Interpreter Mike Jones and some of his colleagues harbor almost mystical feelings. "Superior's moods rule everything. It is unpredictable. You make your plans, but the lake sets your schedule," Mike told me more than once.

Aboard one of the park's workboats, Mike and I made for Otter Cove, in the southern portion of the park. Towing an outboard-powered canoe behind us, we rolled and yawed in the lake's growing swell. The workboat left us with the canoe at Otter Cove, but next morning, when we attempted to head back north, Superior would not let us go far. The swell was so high that it blotted out the horizon when we were in its trough. It was difficult to steer, and the wind was beginning to push us with considerable force.

We ducked out of the storm at Otter Island and from its lighthouse radioed the park boat to come get us. Steaming north, in seas that broke against the dark granite cliffs and sent towers of spray into the sky, we put into a sheltered beach. Next day, in the canoe, we followed a passage to Oiseau Bay. Mike had to return to park headquarters and left me there with an inflatable boat equipped with a small outboard motor.

I spent the next two days exploring crescent-shaped Oiseau Bay. Oiseau is full of inviting beaches and is studded with little islands of variegated, water-smoothed granite. In my solitude, I surrendered to the magnificent setting, enjoying the crash of surf on distant rocks and the dark and silent forest behind the beach.

I followed the park trail for several miles. The forest floor was carpeted with lichens, moist and verdant expanses of mosses, and clusters of ferns. There were blue asters and other flowers and mushrooms growing amid the fallen autumn leaves. Lichens bearded the lower branches of spruce trees; the silver-trunked birches were turning to leafy gold.

My only daytime visitors were chipmunks, a few gulls, and flocks of Canada geese barking noisily high overhead. I found the tracks of my nighttime visitors on the beach each morning: A small bear came by twice, and some otters and other animals whose tracks I could not identify had also passed by.

On the last day, Superior was calm, allowing me to head north in the inflatable boat. The sun sparkled on the lake. The air was chilly and crystalline. As my boat skimmed the nearly flat water beneath the dark and brooding cliffs, Gitche Gumee—the "shining Big-Sea-Water" of *The Song of Hiawatha*—brought to mind another poem of Longfellow's I had learned in childhood:

> *This is the forest primeval. The murmuring pines and*
> *the hemlocks,*
> *Bearded with moss, and in garments green, indistinct*
> *in the twilight. . . .*

The forest at Pukaskwa was indeed primeval, clad in "garments green," crepuscular, mysterious. It was so starkly different from the country I had seen in the north—the windswept tundra that rolled mile upon empty mile from forest's edge to the arctic seas. So different, yet so similar in the feelings it evoked—a sense of wildness, of vastness, of power. Forest and tundra—both are the essence of the great Shield, the untamed heart of Canada, formed of ancient bedrock and forever ruled by nature's elemental forces.

Stands of spruce and jack pine crowd a rock-ribbed island in one of the many coves
along the shoreline of Pukaskwa National Park. Pukaskwa encompasses 725 square miles
of rugged wilderness on the northeast shore of Lake Superior, the world's largest expanse
of fresh water. At left, Pukaskwa bears the fury of an autumn storm as crashing waves explode
against its granite ramparts. The passage of time has left its mark on the tortured rocks of
Pukaskwa, whose variegated patterns (opposite, above), reveal the many changes wrought
by volcanic action and the immense stresses and pressures within the earth.

Rich hues of fallen maple leaves tint the forest floor of Mont Tremblant Provincial Park (left and right). A placid lake in nearby La Mauricie National Park (above) reflects a mist-softened image of woodland splendor. National and provincial parks and wildlife refuges protect portions of the Shield's many and varied environments. In southern Quebec, they provide unique and easily accessible areas of glacier-scoured terrain, mountains, lakes, and hardwood and evergreen forests. La Mauricie offers miles of trails for hikers, skiers, and snowshoers; extensive downhill runs make Mont Tremblant famous for its alpine skiing.

Massed in flight, a blizzard of snow geese swirls above the St. Lawrence River at Cap Tourmente

National Wildlife Area, where scores of thousands of geese stop during their migrations.

Spurred by primal impulses, caribou of the George River herd migrate in northern Quebec near the time of the annual fall rut (top). During this period, male caribou fight to establish dominance (above). Though they may clash fiercely, the animals seldom inflict serious damage. In their migratory travels, caribou cover hundreds of miles of tundra, undeterred by the many rivers and lakes they must cross. After a crossing, a royal stag (right) shakes water from its thick coat. The George River herd, numbering some 374,000 animals, may rank as the world's largest wild caribou herd. Elsewhere on the Canadian Shield, populations of many herds decline because of overhunting and predation by wolves.

The High Arctic

By James Conaway • Photographs by Stephen J. Krasemann

Ice-glazed peaks dwarf Inuit hunters crossing Baffin Island's Pangnirtung Fiord in early spring. For much of the year, savage weather renders nearly all the high Arctic a forbidding fastness.

The High Arctic

"DON'T GET CAUGHT IN THERE when it starts to blow." The words of the Royal Canadian Mounted Police officer came back to me as I listened to the wind howl. Crouched behind a boulder in Pangnirtung Pass, on southern Baffin Island, I looked up at domed clouds hanging about jagged peaks. Massive tongues of ice spilled from the high valleys and from the distant ice caps that can fuel gales of more than a hundred miles an hour. The frozen braids of the Weasel River had been pocked by the wind. Even the black lichens growing here had sought refuge on southward facing rocks.

From the tiny coastal town of Pangnirtung, I had ridden a snowmobile for 19 miles up a frozen fiord, then hiked for three hours across brittle ice pans and rocky rubble pushed up by glaciers. I was with photographer Stephen Krasemann, a wilderness veteran who has traveled in many parts of Canada. The two of us had come to Baffin at the beginning of a two-month journey through the islands of Canada's high Arctic, a sweeping archipelago that at times is one of the cruelest environments on earth.

An austere and unforgiving realm, the Arctic is locked in ice for three-quarters of the year. Here a simple miscalculation, such as an unexpected fall or a soaking, can be fatal. The weather can be harsh at any time of year, and hypothermia—the loss of body heat—can easily kill even in the warmest months. Nearly all the Arctic is in fact a polar desert, receiving no more moisture than the Sahara; an average of less than five inches of snow and rain fall in this region each year. In winter, temperatures can plunge to minus 50°F. This is a land with its own disconcerting rhythms, where the blackness of a winter night can stretch for more than two months.

But despite its forbidding nature, the Arctic is a storehouse of life. Indeed, the barrenness of the land conceals an intricate, interdependent ecological system that was to astonish me with its variety and beauty. During the brief arctic summer, the region opens its doors to the constant sun, offering warmth and sustenance to the tough, versatile animals that during the rest of the year must forage in ice and snow. In summer, when temperatures can reach the mid-60s, swarms of insects appear, myriad flowering plants burst forth, and birds in the hundreds of thousands migrate here to nest. The vast bleakness of the Arctic also harbors mineral resources, including deposits of oil and gas—riches that are attracting the attention of the civilized, consuming world.

Stephen and I planned to visit some of the most beautiful spots in the Arctic Archipelago: distant mountain ranges, hidden valleys, and twisting fiords where few people have ever set foot. We hoped to see plants and animals found nowhere else, and to encounter firsthand an environment that has challenged man for centuries.

Baffin is the largest island in the archipelago—bigger than Sweden. It was not completely mapped until the middle of the 20th century. In 1972 the Canadian government set aside a portion of Baffin's Cumberland Peninsula, later naming it Auyuittuq National Park. Auyuittuq is the only national park north of the Arctic Circle and one that will never be visited by a Winnebago. There are no roads—or few facilities of any kind—within this 8,300-square-mile wilderness. "Visitors here must be self-sufficient," explained superintendent Bob Redhead, "for our rescue capability is extremely limited." It was Auyuittuq that Stephen and I had come to see.

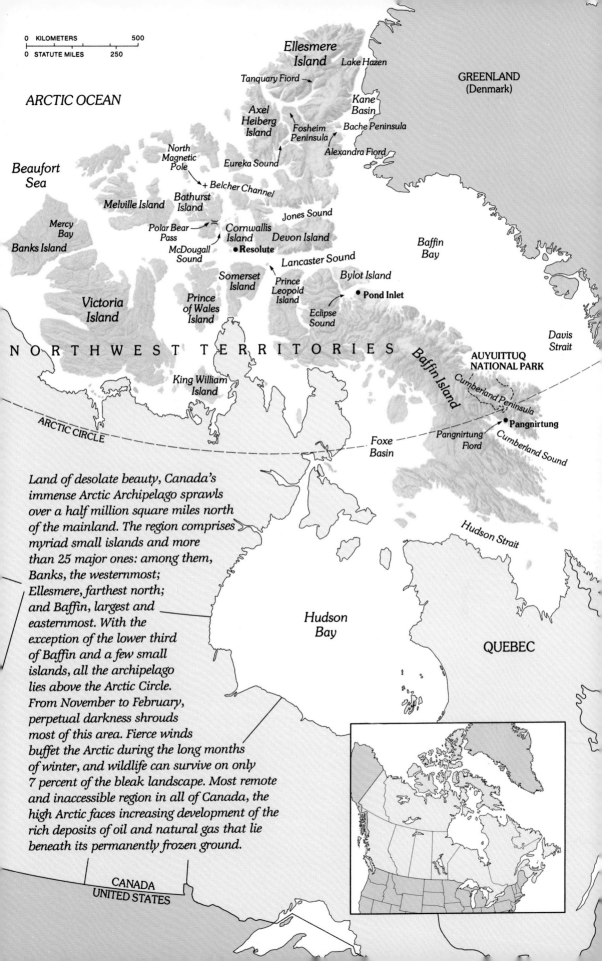

ARCTIC OCEAN

Ellesmere
Island

GREENLAND
(Denmark)

Lake Hazen

Tanquary Fiord

Kane
Basin

Axel
Heiberg
Island

Bache Peninsula

Fosheim
Peninsula

North
Magnetic
Pole

Eureka Sound

Alexandra Fiord

Beaufort
Sea

+ Belcher Channel

Bathurst
Island

Melville Island

Jones Sound

Polar Bear
Pass

Cornwallis
Island

Devon Island

Baffin
Bay

McDougall
Sound

• Resolute

Mercy
Bay

Lancaster Sound

Banks Island

Somerset
Island

Prince
Leopold
Island

Bylot Island

• Pond Inlet

Victoria
Island

Prince
of Wales
Island

Eclipse
Sound

Davis
Strait

N O R T H W E S T   T E R R I T O R I E S

King William
Island

AUYUITTUQ
NATIONAL PARK

Cumberland Peninsula

ARCTIC CIRCLE

Foxe
Basin

Pangnirtung
Fiord

• Pangnirtung

Cumberland Sound

Hudson Strait

Land of desolate beauty, Canada's
immense Arctic Archipelago sprawls
over a half million square miles north
of the mainland. The region comprises
myriad small islands and more
than 25 major ones: among them,
Banks, the westernmost;
Ellesmere, farthest north;
and Baffin, largest and
easternmost. With the
exception of the lower third
of Baffin and a few small
islands, all the archipelago
lies above the Arctic Circle.
From November to February,
perpetual darkness shrouds
most of this area. Fierce winds
buffet the Arctic during the long months
of winter, and wildlife can survive on only
7 percent of the bleak landscape. Most remote
and inaccessible region in all of Canada, the
high Arctic faces increasing development of the
rich deposits of oil and natural gas that lie
beneath its permanently frozen ground.

Hudson
Bay

QUEBEC

CANADA
UNITED STATES

0 KILOMETERS 500
0 STATUTE MILES 250

I was unprepared for the immensity of this arctic threshold, wild beyond anything I had imagined. The Inuit call it Auyuittuq, which means "the land that never melts." Pangnirtung Pass runs through the heart of Auyuittuq National Park, linking Cumberland Sound with Davis Strait. The pass, an awesome corridor of Precambrian rock, has for eons been subject to the relentless assault of wind, water, and ice.

Pausing in our wind-sheltered spot in Pangnirtung Pass, Stephen and I fired up the camp stove. We had come to Baffin in May. Though officially spring, it felt like winter, with the temperature hovering around freezing during the warmest parts of the day. Tiny ice crystals had formed on Stephen's blond beard; my hands were cold and clumsy. But hot tea revived us. Then we shouldered our packs and hiked on, through air so clear that it destroyed all depth perception. Tirokwa Peak, at least three miles away, seemed touchable. We crossed the Arctic Circle as the sun dipped behind the western mountains. We would have no darkness at this time of year, only a long twilight as the sun circled just below the horizon. With summer approaching, the midnight sun would soon wheel overhead, flooding the Arctic with continuous light for weeks.

Before us now, the blue-veined glaciers, slabs of tumbled granite, and wind-sculpted snowdrifts assumed improbable shapes. The pass narrowed. We topped an old moraine—dirt and rock pushed up by a glacier that later retreated—and saw the roofs of emergency shelters set up on the banks of the Weasel River by Parks Canada, which administers Auyuittuq. Clouds had moved into the pass and a light snow had begun to fall by the time we reached the shelters. We broke the ice on the river to get cooking water and found refuge from the rising wind inside one of the plywood huts.

"I wonder what tomorrow will be like," said Stephen, giving voice to my own fear of being confined here either by snow or gales. We ate dinner while the door rattled, both of us weary from the day's trek and from the cold. The water left in my pot had frozen solid before I could get into my sleeping bag. I took my canteen and leather boots in with me, feeling strange to be in bed while it was still light. Through a crack between the wall and floor I could see snow blowing horizontally against the mountain's black base. Lying there, I thought of the words of Bernhard Hantzsch, a German explorer. "Hardly slept, burning headache, cold compresses," he wrote in his journal on May 26, 1911. Hantzsch died a few days later, presumably of trichinosis contracted from raw polar bear meat, having failed in an attempt to travel the west coast of Baffin. The island's size—196,000 square miles—rugged terrain, ice caps, and ice-choked harbors had long frustrated European explorers.

Man first came to the high Arctic thousands of years before the Europeans, traveling from northeast Asia by way of the Bering Strait. Archaeologists have divided the early cultures here into the Arctic Small Tool tradition, named for the small-scale tools and weapons produced by its people, and the Thule culture, named for the region of Greenland where these seagoing hunters' artifacts were first discovered. The Arctic Small Tool tradition lasted from approximately 2500 B.C. to A.D. 1000 in the high Arctic, after which the Thule culture rose to predominance. Today's Inuit are the direct descendants of those early inhabitants.

August snow hastens the end of the growing season for dwarf willows on Banks Island. Winters come early to the high Arctic and often linger well into June.

Arctic's rough symmetry: Photographer Stephen Krasemann records the austere beauty of ice formations known as glacial shear planes in Auyuittuq National Park, on Baffin Island. "We were exploring a glacier one morning and happened onto this gaping wound that aroused our curiosity. We entered cautiously— the jagged ice was very slippery." Internal stresses sheared the ice into these layers; meltwater trickling downward etched the ridges. Shear planes often form in thin ice at the fringes of glaciers.

The Vikings are believed to have visited Baffin as early as the 11th century. The quest for a seaway to the Orient—the fabled Northwest Passage—inspired later explorers. Martin Frobisher reached the southern tip of Baffin in 1576 and collected samples of what was erroneously thought to be gold. Queen Elizabeth held high hopes that this new land would be of immense value.

Frobisher was followed by other Englishmen, including John Davis, William Baffin, and Robert Bylot. Baffin's famous voyage around Baffin Bay in 1616 led to his mistaken conclusion that "there is no passage nor hope of passage" to the north, though in fact the way through the arctic islands was later found to lie just north of Baffin Island, in what is now called Lancaster Sound.

The next morning Stephen and I set out to climb the steep slope below Tirokwa Peak. Our goal was the glacier located there; we wanted a close look at the force that has helped shape the land. Ice scattered at the foot of the glacier made for treacherous walking, and the glacier's deeply fissured walls were too precipitous to scale. Our voices hushed in awe, we entered an ice cave where boulders studded the ceiling like raisins in a monstrous frosted cake. The emerald walls were as smooth as marble.

The cave's cold beauty, that of the towering granite peak from which it crept, and the yawning valley below, all seemed inimical to life. But that evening the sun illuminated the face of Thor Peak, and a pair of Canada geese flew up the pass, early arrivals from among the hordes of migratory birds that return to the Arctic each

Part of the daily struggle for existence, the constant search for food frequently appears in the art of the far north. Inuit craftsmen fashion their art with only basic implements—ax, chisel, file, and sandpaper. Below, a soapstone carving portrays an Inuk killing a polar bear. The artist completed the eight-inch-tall piece by carving a tiny bow and arrow from resilient caribou antler.

year to nest. I noticed other signs of spring: Buds had appeared on the spindly limbs of willows growing close to the ground, and the arctic heather had begun to stretch new branches toward the hard blue sky. The plants grew in the thin layer of soil above the permafrost, which in the Arctic Archipelago ranges between one and two thousand feet in depth.

For the next week, Stephen and I explored Auyuittuq's wild grandeur. The day we left the park the temperature rose dramatically; I had to pause during the hike out and strip off some clothes. Stephen walked on, his figure obscured by heat waves rising from the gravel flats. Alone, I listened to the sounds of the land forming—the whisper of wind, a rock clattering down the face of a moraine, the sharp report of the thawing river, the hiss and groan of glaciers on both sides of Pangnirtung Pass. As I hiked in silence, I reflected on this, my first taste of the Arctic, and I realized that my presence in this stark polar realm accounted for nothing—a thought that was both humbling and exhilarating.

SEVERAL WEEKS LATER Stephen and I crossed McDougall Sound, a thousand feet above the sea. I could see ringed seals poised beside their holes in the ice. When the plane's shadow approached them, they dove into the frigid, blue-black water. Our flight had begun at Resolute, on Cornwallis Island. Resolute is the hub of activities in the high Arctic, and it served as our base of operations. The town provides an important link to civilization for mining and petroleum companies working in the Arctic, as well as for scientists involved in research—from meteorology to archaeology.

Stephen and I were flying toward Bathurst Island; our destination was Polar Bear Pass, named for the animal that migrates through the area in spring and summer. We were on our way to see one of the largest concentrations of mammals and birds in the high Arctic. Polar Bear Pass attracts 53 species of birds and several kinds of mammals, including the arctic fox and the musk-ox. A man who knows as much as anyone about Polar Bear Pass is Stewart Mac-Donald, curator of vertebrate ethology at Canada's National Museum of Natural Sciences. MacDonald was responsible for creating the research station in the pass, and he has been coming to the area nearly every summer since 1968.

"The difference between wilderness here and wilderness elsewhere," he explained to me, "is the relatively small amount of land on which wildlife can exist. Polar Bear Pass is a vital part of the mere 7 percent of arctic land that is supportive of animal life." For that reason, the National Museum of Natural Sciences has been studying the pass and has determined it should be declared an ecological reserve, a wilderness area protected from development.

Among the equipment Stephen and I had brought with us to Polar Bear Pass were two 12-gauge shotguns, to be loaded with slugs. Guns are standard equipment for scientists and other visitors to areas of the Arctic that are home to polar bears. "Polar bears are extremely dangerous," I had been told by Ray Schweinsburg, a biologist who studies the animals for the Northwest Territories Wildlife Service so the bear population can be monitored and appropriate hunting quotas set. Schweinsburg told me that on a recent tagging mission he had approached a drugged bear that had leaped up from the ice and charged him. "If another member of the tagging team had not shot the bear," he said, "I would probably have been mauled and possibly killed."

As our plane banked over Polar Bear Pass, I braced for my first "off-strip" landing. The plane was a Twin Otter, one of the workhorses of the Arctic. Powerful dual-engine craft, Twin Otters can land and take off in the space of a few hundred yards. Ours was equipped with soft, oversize tires to enable it to set down on rocky beaches and open tundra, although it seemed unlikely that anything other than a helicopter could land safely here in the pass.

At the edge of the barren hills below appeared a cluster of low buildings and the bright orange research station set up by the National Museum of Natural Sciences. Gas drums—the sign of man in the Arctic—could be seen near the impromptu airstrip. We came in low, just above stall speed. The wheels touched and then we lunged forward in our seats, the big turboprops reversing and bringing us to a roaring halt.

I climbed out of the plane, glad to feel the gravelly terrain underfoot. It was mid-June, and I could see clusters of budding purple saxifrage, invisible from the air, as well as green willow leaves and ruddy catkins that lent a warm, subtle coloration to the land. Longtailed jaegers circled overhead, and black-and-white snow buntings streaked past, unperturbed by men and their noisy machines.

Within minutes our gear was unloaded and the plane gone, its angry drone replaced by the sound of the wind. Stephen and I were alone, the first team to visit the pass that year. From a promontory we looked out over two frozen lakes known as Hunting Camp and Obloomi. During summer in the Arctic, a tremendous amount of water is released by melting snow. In most areas this water returns directly to the sea, without benefiting the parched land. But in Polar Bear Pass, some of the water is retained by the two shallow lakes and by the many basins surrounding them, creating a true oasis.

We carried our gear to one of the camp's Parcolls—metal frames covered with insulated plastic and equipped with iron-frame beds, where we spread our sleeping bags. I had brought a compass, and I watched in amazement as the needle drifted 180 degrees between east and west. The nearness of the North Magnetic Pole, located just north of Bathurst in Belcher Channel, makes compass navigation in the Arctic extremely unreliable.

Early the next morning I set off toward Bracebridge Inlet to see if Hunting Camp and Obloomi had begun to thaw. A group of brant—small, dark geese—circled over Obloomi. A pair of king eider ducks settled near the shore on a thin strip of open water, the male resplendent with his showy orange-and-red bill.

According to Stewart MacDonald, migratory birds come to Polar Bear Pass from many parts of the world. Birds banded here have turned up in distant areas: brant in Ireland, red-throated loons in Chesapeake Bay in the eastern United States, and knots—a kind of sandpiper—in Scotland and France. During the arctic summer, the birds have less than two months in which to court, nest, hatch their young, and then prepare them for the long flight south.

I climbed above Obloomi and the land looked like desert, with slabs of sandstone heaved upright and covered with lichens. Like most forms of life in the Arctic, lichens (Continued on page 104)

Weary hunter returns home burdened with caribou meat. For this 22-inch-high carving, the artist used centuries-old whalebone from Blacklead Island, a whaling center in the 1800s located in Cumberland Sound. Once abundant for carving, whalebone remains scarce today. Laws enacted in the 1970s strictly control the hunting of whales in Canada.

"The land that never melts," 8,300-square-mile Auyuittuq National Park embraces jagged peaks, massive U-shaped valleys, and majestic fiords. In a relentless cycle of advance and retreat over millions of years, glaciers have gouged this wilderness area straddling the Arctic Circle on the Cumberland Peninsula of Baffin Island. Cutting a jagged swath through the park, 60-mile-long Pangnirtung Pass (opposite and below)—seen here in early spring's dwindling snow—offers dramatic evidence of glacial force in its shattered boulders, steep defiles, and deep valleys. At left, the author pauses on the Arctic Circle beside an inukshuk, one of the stone markers used in Auyuittuq to show safe, accessible trails. Built in human form, such cairns once guided Inuit on their travels.

Powerful male polar bear—king of the Arctic—hunts seals in frigid seas off the rocky northwest coast of Bylot Island. Experts believe that Canada holds two-thirds of the world's estimated 20-25,000 polar bears. The animals spend most of their lives hunting in the sea or on the winter ice, usually venturing inland only in the warmer months. Glaciers cover about half of desolate Bylot Island, designated a federal migratory bird sanctuary and a proposed national park. From Bylot's mountainous interior, one of the island's largest glaciers (above) scours a wide path as it sweeps downhill and plunges sharply into Maud Bight Bay. Large as an ocean liner, an iceberg drifts past the formidable river of ice.

Specks of life on the vast, barren tundra, four Peary's caribou travel through Polar Bear Pass, on Bathurst Island. In the distance, rocks dating from 365 million years ago, when shallow seas covered this area, spike the tundra. The receding seas left behind reefs, which later eroded into these coral-and-algae remnants, arranged in lines and often in unusual shapes. An array of wildlife seeks haven in Polar Bear Pass, a 1,150-square-mile proposed ecological reserve. At right, a young male Peary's caribou trails two bulls. Smallest species of caribou, Peary's caribou live almost exclusively in the high Arctic.

Triumphing over the Arctic's abrading snows, rampaging winds, and short growing season, a dwarf willow shoots forth wiry catkins at Lake Hazen, on Ellesmere Island. The dwarf willow's spreading branches develop roots wherever they touch the ground, helping this common arctic species to prosper in its bleak environment. Opposite: The Arctic's most abundant and earliest bloomer, purple saxifrage brightens the tundra in Polar Bear Pass. Often nestling in rocky fissures, this hardy plant has adaptations that include dense growth and dwarfed size. Penetrating roots give the plant its name, which means "rock breaker."

are tough and compact. Because they grow so slowly—some no more than an inch every thousand years—they help scientists date moraines and glacial debris. These lichens were bright orange, and the only living plants I saw other than fibrous reindeer moss growing between the rocks. I stood looking down into the next valley, doubting my own sight: Two black, woolly beasts foraged at the edge of the· snow, large and mythic in appearance. They were musk-oxen. I approached them slowly, watching them paw for last year's sedge among the snow, and for the new growth of willow and saxifrage. Ragged tufts of hair clung to their coats; their massive horns dipped to slender points.

I knew that musk-oxen must often struggle for survival in this harsh arctic environment. When threatened, a herd may gather in a circular defensive formation that is effective against wolves but pathetically vulnerable to men. The journals of Norwegian explorer Otto Sverdrup and other early explorers contain detailed descriptions of the slaughter of musk-oxen at close range.

The two bulls saw me and stood their ground, rubbing their noses against their forelegs in some instinctive response to danger. I approached close enough to see their cloudy gray eyes and to photograph the magnificent horns, and then I gingerly retreated.

For a week, Stephen and I hiked the pass and the Scoresby Hills to the north. One morning a raven, a rarity in Polar Bear Pass, woke me, and I emerged from the Parcoll to see four Peary's caribou in the nearby riverbed—white apparitions against the monochrome hills, their elegant racks starkly defined. I quickly dressed and pursued them. The caribou were feeding upwind from me, and I was able to creep quite close. They had blunt muzzles and short, sturdy, heavily furred bodies, grayish white except for the saddles, which were tan. Their splayed hooves seemed too big in proportion to their bodies, as did their gracefully bowed antlers.

The caribou saw me and trotted away with a stiff-legged gait, tails held high. I sat down, and they began to browse again. To my amazement they were soon coming back in my direction, downwind now, and wary. The youngest bull approached within 60 feet, snuffling the breeze, too curious to heed my scent. It took the sound of my camera shutter to send him and his friends racing away.

A fox climbed the steep embankment across the river. Hunting hard, he crisscrossed the ridge, his nose to the ground. An eager consumer of birds' eggs and fledglings, the arctic fox also eats lemmings, and in winter he follows polar bears for miles out onto the sea ice, feeding on seal carcasses the bears abandon.

I crossed the river and walked north, toward a series of small buttes. I climbed one and discovered bits of lemming fur and ptarmigan feathers strewn about, the remains of some raptor's feasts. The face of the cliff concealed an aerie. I inched forward over the crumbling rock. Suddenly a bird screamed above me, and I looked up at the stomach and white underwings of a male rough-legged hawk. The female shot outward from the cliff, adding screams of disapproval to her mate's. Watching me over her shoulder, she gained altitude and then circled back to deal with the intruder, being larger and more aggressive than the male. I retreated, not wanting to further disturb the nesters, and returned to camp.

We had arranged for the plane to pick us up the next day. I had not seen the creature for which the pass was named, but then bears, like people, are transients in Polar Bear Pass. I had, however, seen many of the animals that live here all year, and some of the birds that arrive by the thousand to nest on the tundra, in the rocks, and among the water-filled basins.

I tried to imagine what the pass would look like supporting a pipeline, one proposal that has been made by an energy consortium. Pipelines to transport oil and gas from the Arctic are among many plans for development being put forward. Perhaps the most controversial is the Arctic Pilot Project, a plan involving several energy companies seeking to transport liquefied natural gas through icebound Lancaster Sound in special icebreaking freighters.

Speculation about a year-round shipping lane, and about the effects of possible pollution from oil spills, has placed most Canadians firmly on one side or the other of the question of arctic development. Stewart MacDonald asserts there is "...a ground swell of public opinion against development of these fragile, life-supporting areas." He has written, "The Arctic is a land in danger. It is threatened by commercial scramblings to grab a share of the treasure at the top of the world."

FROM BATHURST ISLAND, Stephen and I returned to Resolute. Resolute was named for the ship of Sir Edward Belcher, leader of a British naval party sent in search of the ill-fated Franklin expedition. Sir John Franklin and 129 shipmates sailed into Lancaster Sound in 1845 while searching for the Northwest Passage. Their ship later became trapped in the ice near King William Island, and all on board perished. No sign of the ship was ever found by the expeditions that followed.

After two days resupplying and organizing our equipment, Stephen and I were ready to head out again, this time due north, to Ellesmere Island. Nearly 500 miles long, Ellesmere is the third largest of the arctic islands—after Baffin and Victoria—and the most mountainous. Protected by mountain ranges from cold winds off the polar ice pack, and subject to unusually long periods of sunny weather, Ellesmere receives summer several weeks before more southerly islands do.

The day we left Resolute, our Twin Otter strained upward from the runway with a load that included a collapsible boat and a motor, extra equipment for another expedition already in the field, and four passengers. We were aboard a flight chartered by the Polar Continental Shelf Project—a government agency that coordinates logistical support for groups involved in arctic research.

I watched Devon Island pass beneath us, only partially thawed in late June. Devon's ice was replaced by the midnight blue of the ocean in Jones Sound. Here the current had created a polynya— open water that harbors wildlife, including whales and walruses. The narrow walls of Hell Gate were easily recognizable from the description written by Otto Sverdrup, who contributed most to the map of Ellesmere. We flew directly over Goose Fiord, where Sverdrup was trapped by ice in 1901 and forced to spend another year in the Arctic—his fourth since leaving Norway—in his ship, the *Fram*.

As I looked down, I thought about the hazards of flying in this hostile region. Airplanes must cross vast stretches of water, ice cap, and mountain, with fuel caches and a radio beam often their only links to survival. There are no alternative airports for pilots who have ventured aloft and find their destination blanketed by clouds or fog. The work is physically demanding, with frequent refueling stops and 20-hour days common. "But it's worth it," pilot Ken Birss had told me in Resolute. "We don't have somebody leading us around by the nose, and we work in fantastic country. You can't imagine the sensation of flying on a winter night when it's 40 below zero outside, and the moon and the northern lights are out. I get a lump in my throat thinking about it."

The high, distant snowfields of Axel Heiberg Island rose on the left, matched by the rugged, snow-draped peaks of southern Ellesmere. Range upon range extended to both horizons, under an endless mantle of ice. Our plane seemed to hang like a mote in the pure arctic air, without movement or significance.

After several hours we dipped down over Eureka Sound, flying a couple of hundred feet above the surface of the melting ice. The wing-tank fuel gauges, which I could see from my seat, registered empty. Suddenly I thought of the ton of cargo that would come careering forward in a crash; it was less reassuring to think of plunging into the near-freezing water, where a person's survival time is something under two minutes. We crossed a gravel cape, low enough to see arctic hare racing away from us. I was relieved to see a dirt runway and the cluster of prefabricated structures that were occupied by the Canadian Army. I asked our present pilot, Paddy Doyle, why he had flown so low over the water. "Just looking for a place to fish," he said with a big Irish grin.

After a brief refueling stop—during which I gratefully learned that the airplane's main tank had held an ample reserve of fuel—we were once again airborne. Our destination was Tanquary Fiord, near the northern end of Ellesmere, where the mountains slip into the sea and three broad valleys come together in one of the most spectacular settings in the Arctic.

Some years before, the Defence Research Board of Canada had established a field camp on the MacDonald River near Tanquary

Arctic hares spring across the lichen-strewn summertime tundra of Ellesmere Island. The arctic hare's fur affords excellent camouflage in winter, while its thickly padded paws provide insulation from the piercing cold. Among the arctic hare's enemies: snowy owls, gyrfalcons, and wolves. A tundra wolf (opposite) stands alert on a hillside. Long, thick fur and the ability to go for days without food help these wolves survive the rigors of arctic life.

Fiord. As we came in for a landing now, we could see Parcolls, a Quonset hut, and a row of neat white tents. The tents were housing a group of geologists working for Petro-Canada. The scientists, we learned, were searching for mineral deposits here on Ellesmere.

Stephen and I pitched our tents on the beach by the fiord and accepted the group's invitation to dinner. Among the party was

Dr. Bill Kerr, a geologist. Kerr has been coming to the Arctic in the summer for 26 years. After a supper of steak and apple pie, he told us about visiting Bathurst Island in the early 1960s. "I was at Bathurst in August, and I saw bears migrating through the pass, after the ice had broken up. The pass didn't have a name, so I called it Polar Bear Pass." The name stuck.

A day or two after our arrival at Tanquary, Stephen and I climbed into a Petro-Canada helicopter for a flight up the valley of the Rollrock River. Here the mountains pulled back, and the combined melt from the Viking and Ad Astra Ice Caps flooded the plain for miles. The awesome power of the glaciers was visible from the air: They scraped and gouged the valley, pushing along tons of rock. Dazzlingly white on the surface, the glaciers crept from the ice caps like tentacles, thousands of years of compacted snow traveling with a tremendous force.

We flew over Scylla Glacier; on the other side lay the broad valley of the Lewis River. Metallic yellow arctic poppies swayed in the wind, mixed among the purple saxifrage, willow, and myriad yellow-and-white bursts of mountain avens. On the tundra slopes beside the Lewis River, a herd of musk-oxen grazed, the calves miniature versions of the adults, with the same calm dignity. On the other side of the river stood a solitary bull, up to his stomach in grass. Unlike the musk-oxen on Bathurst, he ran when he saw us, his great hump of black hair trembling comically.

Stephen and I spent nearly a week exploring the wild environs of Tanquary Fiord. One day, while stopped for lunch, I dipped my pot into a pond and set it on the pack stove. A big yellow bumblebee wheeled past. Ruddy turnstones stalked at the water's edge, and two arctic hares crouched, black-tipped ears flat against their backs. These 12-to-15-pound hares looked like more than a match for a fox. They hopped, revealing long, muscular, downy white bodies. I stood up, and a surprising thing happened: The hares also rose on their hind legs. They lunged forward with a kind of hopping, running motion, heads held high for a better view of danger, then sprinted away among the rocks.

On another occasion, while resting beside a small stream, I saw something white move on the slope across from me. Large and purposeful, it descended in a straight line toward the stream. It was a seldom-glimpsed tundra wolf. The wolf leaped the stream and trotted toward me across the gravel flats on long, lanky legs. Unlike other wolves I'd seen, it had small, peaked ears and a short muzzle, adaptations to reduce heat loss in its frigid environment. The wolf stopped to pick up a piece of hare carcass, his eyes seemingly fixed in my direction. I could hear the bones crack between his teeth.

He came on. I knew that wolves do not usually attack people, but this one was uncomfortably close. I moved, and the wolf turned and loped off down the valley.

To the northeast of our camp at Tanquary lay Lake Hazen, in the shadow of the snow-covered mountains of northern Ellesmere. The Lake Hazen basin was said to form another—and the northernmost—arctic oasis, with unusual plant life and breathtaking terrain. The lake is fed by the Very River and by the many torrents from the Garfield Range to the northwest. Flying in from Tanquary, we circled over gas drums set out on (Continued on page 116)

Tranquillity overspreads the pageant of birdlife at Lake Hazen, a wilderness oasis marked by unusually high summer temperatures and vigorous plant growth. At right, four rock ptarmigan chicks snuggle close to their mother, concealed by plumage that will turn white before winter. A male king eider duck, distinguished in the breeding season by the bright orange nodule above his beak, paddles leisurely with his mate across a meltwater pond (left). Marshy grasses at water's edge provide a comfortable nesting site for a red-throated loon (top). Above, another loon settles over her two spotted eggs. She will warm the eggs until they hatch in about four weeks.

On distant Ellesmere Island, clouds drift across peaks of Canada's northernmost chain, known as

the Grant Land Mountains. Most of these mountains lie buried under a perpetual shroud of ice.

Nesting, gathering food, and raising young fill the long daylight hours of summer for birds of the tundra. Arching its wings, a long-tailed jaeger on Ellesmere hovers in midair (left); elongated tail feathers function as a rudder. Seen throughout the arctic islands, jaegers spend most of their lives at sea, coming ashore only to nest and to hunt. At bottom, an arctic fox in pursuit of a meal endures a jaeger's threatening swoops, a tactic the bird uses to defend its nest or simply to harass an unwelcome intruder. Sharing responsibilities, a watchful pair of jaegers prepares to feed a morsel of predigested food to their fuzzy, hours-old chick (below).

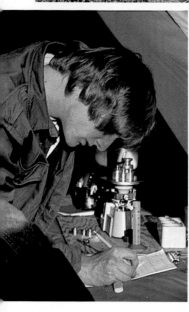

Plume of water jets from a glacier along the east coast of Ellesmere. Beyond, meltwater channels at the foot of the glacier thread sinuously toward mountain-rimmed Alexandra Fiord. Unusual in the Arctic, glacial geysers occur where the weight of ice creates great pressure, forcing underlying water to the surface through crevasses. At Alexandra Fiord, lush plant growth, supported by warm summers and sufficient moisture, challenges an 11-member ecology team. The group hopes to determine the conditions necessary for certain plant communities to flourish in the Arctic. Tests include measurements of soil and air temperatures, wind speed and direction, and radiation levels. At left, climatologist George Reynolds adjusts a sensor on a meteorological station set up in a meadow, while entomologist Olga Kukal records data. In the nearby tent, graduate student Greg Henry (opposite, lower) weighs pieces of sod to determine the rate of water loss that occurs in 24 hours.

the northern shore of the lake, where the Defence Research Board had set up a camp in 1957. The camp was now being used as a base for naturalists studying the numerous plant species that thrive along Lake Hazen's 48-mile length and in the surrounding hills.

When we landed, we were met by Dr. Josef Svoboda, associate professor of botany at the Erindale Campus of the University of Toronto. With him were two of his students. I asked where I should pitch my tent. Svoboda swept an open palm across tundra dotted with purple saxifrage and the bright yellow cinquefoil. "Pick a spot," he said with his soft Czech accent. Svoboda and his team were using a Quonset hut as a combination research center, mess hall, and social center. The area around the hut was strewn with bits of equipment left by various expeditions years before. Pots and pans, bits of machinery, even a duffel bag, bore little signs of deterioration after more than two decades of exposure in the cold, dry air.

Next morning I accepted an invitation to join Svoboda and two of his students on a trek into the hills to search for plant specimens. "We believe northern Ellesmere harbored refugia—areas untouched by the masses of ice that scraped the rest of the land during the periods of ice age glaciation," Svoboda said. "One possible indication of this is a tiny willow herb discovered here."

The willow herb had been found in the foothills of the Garfield Range, and Svoboda wanted to mark the plant for future study. As we hiked across the tundra we passed blooming dandelions, bell-like bladder campion, prickly saxifrage, and yellow, woolly lousewort, with fernlike stalks and dense crowns of flowers. Svoboda pointed out each plant with the care of a trained scientist and the delight of an enthusiast who had spent years studying the flora and fauna of his adopted region. "There is beauty in the Arctic," said Svoboda, "but sometimes you have to look closely to find it.

"Most of the high Arctic flowering plants are believed to be of alpine origin, and therefore are not fully adapted to arctic conditions. They require a period of heat every summer to flower and produce seeds." Svoboda explained that most of the plants grow in a "boundary layer"—the first few centimeters above ground, where the air is as much as three times warmer than the air higher up.

We climbed a steep valley and found the willow herb Svoboda sought—a tiny purple stalk with a delicate white blossom. We drove a stake into the ground and tied a piece of red plastic ribbon to it so the plant could be relocated. "This plant may not seem like much," Svoboda said, "but it is important, indicating that parts of upper Ellesmere could have been ice-free and warm enough for the herb to have survived during the ice ages."

From Lake Hazen Stephen and I flew to Sverdrup Pass, which cuts across Ellesmere Island from east to west, a broad, deep valley hemmed in by snowcapped mountains. Flying toward the pass, I watched the brown plain of the Fosheim Peninsula rise into creased and folded mountains, fast in the grip of ice. Rivers carrying mud created dark, cloud-like formations in the bays and fiords. Cracks showed in the high snowfields, where the color shaded from gray to pale blue to a flat white that made altitude perception difficult. Glaciers etched with dark concentric lines tumbled down the south slopes toward the pass. Meltwater plunged a thousand feet from a cleft in the mountainside to the shattered rock below.

Our pilot, the inquisitive Paddy Doyle, flew in low around the stony headland of Thorvald Peninsula. The ice had disappeared from the shore and was beginning to melt out in the bay. We landed on the tundra behind an abandoned Royal Canadian Mounted Police post at Alexandra Fiord. The post was being used with the permission of the Mounted Police to house scientists and graduate students working in the valley.

As we unloaded our gear, I could sense that the arctic summer had already begun to wane. The mountain aven blooms were now straw-like, and the stems of heather were turning brown. Mosquitoes tapped against the tent fabric with greater urgency. The other sounds—running water, birdcalls, the crack of ice—all suggested that the Arctic was hurrying to complete the short cycle of life before the inevitable freeze.

After setting up my tent, I chatted with the scientists and students here at Alexandra Fiord. George Reynolds, a climatologist, explained the weather at "Alex," as the station is called. "The mass of cool air above Greenland, the Greenland High, keeps the skies clear," he said. "The clouds that form over the open water of Kane Basin dissipate before reaching the protected lowland of Alexandra Fiord. It's a classic desert situation here of low precipitation and abundant sunshine."

Olga Kukal, an entomologist, told me that there are many insects in the Arctic. "Gnats, flies, midges, wasps, even moths and butterflies. The insects are as opportunistic as the mammals, feeding on whatever is available."

The next morning I set off across the tundra to explore the hills behind our camp. I had slept only a few hours, but the constant sunlight seemed to lessen the need for sleep. A hundred yards back from the fiord, away from the cooling ice, the temperature rose considerably. Young snow buntings flew awkwardly from rock to rock, and a female jaeger hopped away, trailing a wing on the ground to distract me from two oval, spotted eggs in her nest.

Butterflies and moths flitted along the ground. I climbed past granite boulders, some the color of salmon, shot through with feldspar. Garnets and quartz studded the massive chunks of sandstone that lay about. A ptarmigan hen flew up almost from beneath my foot, revealing her nest and eight speckled eggs. She settled a few yards away, almost invisible in her mottled summer plumage.

In the next valley a glacier dipped so gradually to the ground that I could have easily stepped onto it. I could have hiked miles to the ice cap, but I wanted to climb the rocky crown overlooking the fiord. The islands below were reflected in the puddled ice, as if in an antique mirror. An iceberg the size of a cathedral floated regally in the distant, bright blue water, a calf off one of the huge glaciers farther north that send icebergs down into Baffin Bay and the North Atlantic. Beyond the open water lay Greenland.

One of the scientists at Alex told of seeing evidence of prehistoric encampments along the coast to the east. The following day I decided to search for these signs of human habitation. I hiked eastward, wading a shallow river while arctic terns dove at me, protecting their nests on the sandy bank. I scrambled over a rocky point to a marshy isthmus near sea level. There I found rings of stone set in oblong patterns, showing where skin tents had once been set up by

Remains of an ancient dwelling on Bylot Island intrigue Murray McComb, a senior planner with Parks Canada. The whale skull in the foreground probably supported the entrance tunnel of the semisubterranean house. From about A.D. 1000 till 1500, people of the Thule culture, ancestors of today's Inuit, wintered in the high Arctic in such houses.

hunting parties during arctic man's prehistory. Much evidence of man's early presence on Ellesmere has been discovered in the area of nearby Bache Peninsula. Some of these discoveries were made by Peter Schledermann, director of the Arctic Institute of North America. He has recorded evidence of early encampments along Ellesmere's eastern coast, and on Skraeling Island, located within view of our camp at Alexandra Fiord.

Schledermann was again on Ellesmere doing archaeological research, and I was able to talk with him by radio. He explained to me that for thousands of years the winter sea ice has provided a bridge that enables migrating hunters to cross back and forth between Greenland and Ellesmere. Schledermann has found sites on Ellesmere that indicate man was living there more than 4,000 years ago. He has also discovered evidence that 12th-century Viking explorers may have landed on Ellesmere, which is some 500 miles farther north than previously thought.

Later, as I prepared to leave Ellesmere, I tried to visualize what it would be like to spend the winter here, as those early inhabitants had done. I found myself marveling at the tenacity of a people able to exist on this beautifully bleak coast, but I was glad that I would be far to the south when the savage gales of winter began to blow.

BYLOT ISLAND WAS TO BE my last stop in the Arctic. Located off the northern tip of Baffin Island, Bylot has been designated a bird sanctuary by the Canadian government. The island, a majestic mass of alpine peaks and ice fields, rises like a frosted granite column from the sea. Vertical cliffs on the eastern and northern sides of Bylot provide a haven for the thick-billed murres and black-legged kittiwakes that nest there in the thousands, high above the tides. On the rocky shore west of Cape Hay, polar bears forage, while out in the inky blue water of Lancaster Sound belugas rise and fall in ghostly precision, herding putty-gray calves among them.

On the way to Bylot Island I flew to Pond Inlet, a town on the northern shore of Baffin Island across from Bylot. There in the Co-op Hotel I met Boaz Idlaut, a 21-year-old Inuk who is typical of his generation: He enjoys eating Inuit delicacies, such as raw seal meat and the dried skin of the narwhal, but he also likes candy bars, freeze-dried beef Stroganoff, and the apple pie served in the hotel.

Boaz agreed to accompany me to Bylot and to act as my guide in a search for the greater snow geese that breed on the flatlands on Bylot's southwest shore. A helicopter flew us across Eclipse Sound. We camped near the sound on tundra slopes, above a deep, fast-flowing river. The sky was gray and spitting rain, with tattered clouds riding in from the east out of Baffin Bay.

The first day we saw no geese, only long-tailed jaegers, ravens, and glaucous gulls. The wind was blowing so hard when we returned to camp that we had to anchor our tents with stones hauled up from the river. We cooked our freeze-dried food huddled on the leeward side of my tent, pelted by the drizzle.

The rain had stopped by morning, but the sky was still overcast when we set off toward the sound. I carried binoculars to spot the elusive snow geese, now unable to fly because of their molting. Boaz saw the geese first—white specks moving across the tundra with amazing speed. Snow geese have keen eyesight and are cautious, as heavily hunted birds usually are. We stalked the geese in the valleys, but when we emerged on the beach they were already swimming out into the sound, herding their goslings before them.

Evidence of arctic man lay around us: blackened bits of driftwood where a fire once provided warmth, and an ancient lichen-covered whalebone left here by hunters long ago. Boaz dug his hand into the silt at the bottom of a stream and brought up the rib of a narwhal. Today they are killed for their tusks, hunted from power-boats with rifles and shotguns. Every year they swim in schools close to the shore, more afraid of the killer whale than of man. "They make so much noise breathing," said Boaz, "that you can hear them a half mile away."

We hiked in a huge circle that took us into the foothills of the Byam Martin Mountains, but we saw no more geese. A pair of red-throated loons flew in low over a pond and landed in long graceful glides. Golden plovers circled us, crying out as if they held us responsible for the bad weather.

We returned to camp and prepared dinner. The wind that had been blowing stopped while we ate; our parkas were soon covered with mosquitoes. Large, cumbersome, and persistent, they drove us into our respective tents. I tried to read but was distracted by the knowledge that I would soon be leaving the high Arctic.

I was awakened after midnight by the strange, drawn-out call of the loon. The night had grown cooler. The clouds—and the mosquitoes—had disappeared. I stepped from the tent, and a lemming scurried across the tundra to its burrow. The sun lit up the icebergs floating out in the sound like great white frigates. The river gorge below, carpeted with arctic poppies, white mountain avens, and lavender willow herb, glowed in the soft light.

Standing there, I realized how much the beauty of the Arctic had exceeded my expectations. This land had proved to be more than ice, snow, and rock. I had seen a variety and complexity of life—from the lowliest lichen clinging to a boulder to the breeding rituals of migratory birds—that was continuously a surprise and a delight. In the Arctic's vast solitude I had found an enduring strength. That strength was symbolized now by the ice-covered mountains before me: On this arctic night, those distant peaks remained as they have always been—whole and indomitable.

Lithe sea mammals, four streamlined adult belugas and two calves cruise shallow waters off the northern shores of Somerset Island. Each July and August, herds of the white whales gather in this quiet cove for calving. At left, an inquisitive beluga emerges for a better view. Air breathers, belugas must migrate before the surface ice becomes too thick to penetrate. Still, entrapment by the ice means death for some each season. Ice breakup caused by warm weather clogs seas around Prince Leopold Island (right), adjacent to the northeast corner of Somerset. Gale-force winds often lash this desolate column of land, where colonies of murres, glaucous gulls, and numerous other seabirds nest on the nearly vertical 800-to-1,000-foot limestone cliffs. Polynyas—ice-free pockets of water just offshore—attract polar bears, whales, and seals to this area.

Eroded ice masses form a bizarre sculpture garden in Mercy Bay, an inlet along northern Banks

Island. A proposed 3,300-square-mile national park includes the bay and a section of the island.

*Ice Age survivors: Musk-oxen on Banks Island calmly weather
an arctic snowstorm, just as these shaggy creatures have done for
millennia. Thick coats, hooves suited for climbing, and eyes able to
adjust to the low light of winter and to summer's harsh glare help
equip these animals for their lives on remote arctic ranges. Whenever
danger threatens, musk-oxen crowd together with their young
bunched between the adults. Despite its curiosity, a calf stays close
to its mother (right). Musk-oxen herds on Banks have increased
rapidly—to an estimated 20,000 animals—as a result of the dense
plant life and the scarcity of predators there. Local Inuit fear the
herds could soon exceed available grazing lands, threatening both
the musk-oxen's survival and that of the Peary's caribou that share
their environment. At far right, stands of autumn-tinged dwarf
willow, a favorite food of musk-oxen, cover a field near Mercy Bay.*

The Interior Plains

By Thomas O'Neill · Photographs by Paul von Baich

Gnarled badlands of Dinosaur Provincial Park cut deep into the rolling prairie of the interior plains. This eroded terrain in southern Alberta contains one of the richest dinosaur fossil beds in the world.

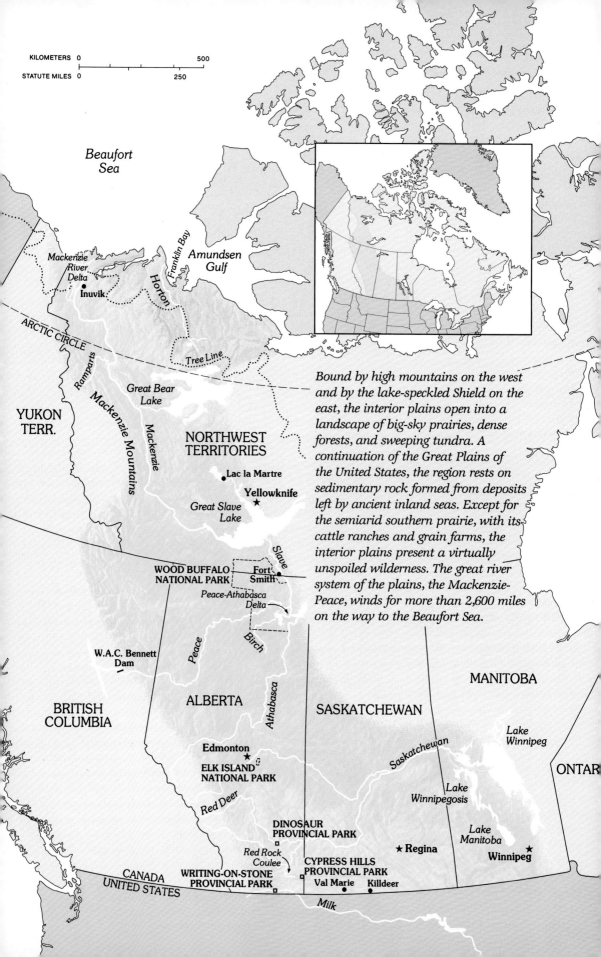

KILOMETERS 0   500
STATUTE MILES 0   250

*Beaufort
Sea*

*Mackenzie
River
Delta*

Inuvik

Franklin Bay

*Amundsen
Gulf*

ARCTIC CIRCLE

Ramparts

Horton

Tree Line

*Great Bear
Lake*

Mackenzie Mountains

Mackenzie

**YUKON
TERR.**

**NORTHWEST
TERRITORIES**

● **Lac la Martre**

★ **Yellowknife**

*Great Slave
Lake*

Slave

**WOOD BUFFALO
NATIONAL PARK**

**Fort
Smith** ●

*Peace-Athabasca
Delta*

Birch

**W.A.C. Bennett
Dam**

Peace

**BRITISH
COLUMBIA**

ALBERTA

Athabasca

SASKATCHEWAN

MANITOBA

*Lake
Winnipeg*

ONTAR

Edmonton ★

**ELK ISLAND
NATIONAL PARK**

Saskatchewan

*Lake
Winnipegosis*

Red Deer

**DINOSAUR
PROVINCIAL PARK**

*Lake
Manitoba*

★ **Regina**

Winnipeg ★

*Red Rock
Coulee*

**CYPRESS HILLS
PROVINCIAL PARK**

**WRITING-ON-STONE
PROVINCIAL PARK**

Val Marie ●   **Killdeer** ●

**CANADA
UNITED STATES**

Milk

Bound by high mountains on the west
and by the lake-speckled Shield on the
east, the interior plains open into a
landscape of big-sky prairies, dense
forests, and sweeping tundra. A
continuation of the Great Plains of
the United States, the region rests on
sedimentary rock formed from deposits
left by ancient inland seas. Except for
the semiarid southern prairie, with its
cattle ranches and grain farms, the
interior plains present a virtually
unspoiled wilderness. The great river
system of the plains, the Mackenzie-
Peace, winds for more than 2,600 miles
on the way to the Beaufort Sea.

SOMETIME IN THE MIDDLE OF THE NIGHT the wind let up. The sudden stillness awoke us. We were camped on the open tundra, our tents huddled in a stand of low willows. Quickly we collapsed the tents, gathered our gear. Before long we had slid the silvery canoe back into the dark waters of the river. As mist rolled past us like hurrying spirits, we looked for the swan, the one that several times had appeared on the water far in front of our canoe, keeping the same distance as if leading us to a special point. But the swan had vanished.

The Interior Plains

In the chill air we paddled hard, glad to return to the current. For almost two days, wind and rain had pinned photographer Paul von Baich and me to a campsite on a high bank of the Horton River, in Canada's Northwest Territories. Bare hills rose behind us. We had passed the tree line three days earlier as we paddled north toward Amundsen Gulf. The month was July, and where we were, some 175 miles above the Arctic Circle, the sun never set. At night it circled above the horizon like a restless sleepwalker.

In such a state we abandoned any notions of day and night. Without the constraint of darkness we ended up timing our movements by the wind, the dominant presence of our journey on the Horton. Gusts from the northwest threw whitecaps on the river, forcing us to drop to our knees in the canoe to reduce wind resistance. Easterly winds dispelled the cold that left frost on our tents and helped push our craft along at an increased speed. The wind ushered in the clouds, hurled up dust storms, lulled us to sleep.

On this white arctic night we took advantage of the rare pause in the wind. Floating through the veil of mist, we rounded a bend and in the dim light saw two wolf cubs on the shore, watching us. On the other side of the river a pale full moon crested the hills, while directly above it, through the torn fog, burned the sun. The wolves bounded away into the brush as the mist obscured sun and moon. The canoe glided silently downriver. It was an enchanted moment, a gift of the wind.

Paul and I covered 25 miles that day—our eleventh on the Horton—paddling until our arms became leaden. This far north even the meager stands of willows we had seen earlier were becoming scarce, and we considered ourselves lucky to find a thin scattering of bushes to serve as a windbreak for our camp that night.

We would not move for the next three days: Overnight the northwest wind rose again and tore at our tents in gusts stronger than any we had experienced before on the river. The cold, damp weather stiffened Paul's back, and he could walk only with great difficulty, using a paddle for a cane. Weather-bound in a remote campsite above the tree line, with little to do save burrow into a sleeping bag or cast a fly into the agitated river, I found time to reflect on what had brought us to this isolated spot.

Paul, a black-bearded veteran of the western Canadian woods, and I, who had learned to canoe on rivers in Maryland and Virginia, had come together for a summer to sample the wilds of Canada's interior plains. Our territory took in a vast swath of land bound on the west by sharp-spined mountain ranges, and on the east by the lake-pocked bedrock of the Canadian Shield. A continuation of the Great Plains of the United States, the interior plains stretch from the U. S.-Canadian border to the Arctic Ocean.

Scientists believe a succession of inland seas submerged part or all of this low-lying region beginning about 600 million years ago. The last sea retreated some 65 million years ago. These warm, shallow bodies of water left behind thick deposits of sand, shale, and lime that over time hardened into rock. The much older and harder rock of the Canadian Shield is unseen in the interior plains, buried by a sedimentary mantle as much as 10,000 feet thick.

During our travels in the plains, Paul and I were to see this region in its many guises: grasslands reaching toward the horizon, dense forests of spruce and pine, labyrinthine marshes, and open tundra. Except for the southern prairie, with its mosaic of farms and towns, the plains region remains an immense wilderness.

Paul and I had chosen to explore the northernmost part of this region first, during the brief, two-month-long arctic summer, which begins here in July. Our trip began with a flight to the town of Inuvik, located on the Mackenzie River Delta, just south of the Arctic Ocean. As we flew over the northern plains, I was amazed by the amount of water I saw standing on the land. We looked down on a landscape so spotted with lakes that it reminded me of puddles on a cobblestone lane. Every few miles there appeared a scribble of a river as well. The great river of the interior plains is the Mackenzie, which flows more than a thousand miles, from Great Slave Lake to the Beaufort Sea, making it one of the longest rivers in Canada. With its tributaries, the river drains some 700,000 square miles, an area larger than Alaska. This vast river system is second in extent in North America only to the Mississippi-Missouri.

Of the many rivers we could have traveled in this northern land, Paul and I chose the Horton for the adventure it offered. While the mile-wide Mackenzie serves as a busy transportation route for barges carrying fuel oil and other heavy freight to arctic settlements, the Horton exists at the other extreme—remote and unused. Hardly more than a handful of people have canoed it at any length. In Inuvik we had difficulty finding a pilot who was willing to land on this little known river.

The Horton was discovered in 1826 by Dr. John Richardson, a British surgeon. He sailed by the river's mouth while on a reconnaissance trip for Capt. John Franklin, who was searching for the Northwest Passage. Richardson named the river for Wilmot Horton, a deskbound under secretary of state back in London. The river was not explored, however, until the early 20th century, when Vilhjálmur Stefánsson, a noted chronicler of Inuit culture, and Rudolph Anderson, a zoologist, traveled much of its length during their 1908-1912 expedition.

Besides its pristine nature, the 330-mile-long Horton offers a dramatic contrast in the midst of the flat arctic plain. The sinuous river has incised its route through soft shale and sandstone to create an impressive valley several hundred feet deep. Terraced cliffs, some as green as an Irish hillside, extend back from the banks of the river, and the environs are populated with a rich variety of wildlife. Because of these attributes, Parks Canada has surveyed the Horton and deemed it a potential site for a national park.

After four days in Inuvik, Paul and I were finally able to find a pilot who would fly us to the Horton, 200 miles to the east. The midnight sun glazed the river as we disengaged our 17-foot aluminum canoe from one of the plane's floats. Alone, we watched as the plane circled back toward Inuvik. Shortly afterward a moose and its calf emerged from the spruce forest and crossed the river. "Looks like a camel," Paul said in an accent born of Yugoslavia and Austria, where he spent his youth. Indeed, from that instant, many things would appear exotic on this distant, hill-enclosed river.

As Paul and I traveled the Horton, we often saw ourselves as privileged witnesses of the wilderness. But other moments came that made us feel like intruders. One day, as we passed a high stony

bluff, two peregrine falcons began to wheel above us. We were excited to glimpse these rare birds of prey. An endangered species, the peregrine nests along the cliffs of the northern end of the Horton, though the number of nests there has decreased from 15 to 5 between 1968 and 1975, according to a government survey.

The peregrines were not keen to see us, however. We had obviously trespassed into the vicinity of the birds' aerie, and the female, the more aggressive of the two, started to swoop down on us, emitting a strident *kek-kek-kek*. We ducked instinctively and heard the whoosh of air as the falcon pulled out of its dive only a few feet above our heads. While the female buzzed us repeatedly, the male circled far above, not once silencing its cry. This behavior persisted for a very long 400 yards, until we moved out of the nesting area.

Unlike the peregrine falcons, the large herbivores of the tundra—the caribou and the musk-ox—seemed curious to see us. Once we surprised a large caribou bull that was standing in a distinguished pose on a gravel bar. He was traveling apart from the herd, as older males do during the summer. We approached upwind, and the caribou, crowned with a candelabrum-like rack, edged closer for a look. He came to within 40 yards of us, then quickly trotted back a few steps before turning to stare. He repeated this routine two or three times. Finally the caribou sensed some danger, or perhaps just lost interest, and swam across the river with

Spared the plow, a lush mixed-grass prairie thrives in southern Alberta. The Sweet Grass Hills of Montana crown the far horizon. Overgrazing and cultivation have claimed much of Canada's prairie, yet a few large tracts of virgin grasslands remain. Federal officials hope to open the first grasslands national park by 1988, in Saskatchewan.

his head and his peculiar-looking mast visible above the water.

Another time, during an off-river hike, we came face to face with a musk-ox. We traded stares with the large, humped beast after it abruptly appeared on a knoll about 30 feet above us. It resembled an evolutionary throwback, with its hairy face and its forbidding brow and horns. Its long coat shivered in the wind. Protected from hunting since 1917, Canada's musk-oxen have recently begun to increase in number and to extend their range. Their population in the region north of Great Bear Lake today totals an estimated 2,000. After apparently assuring itself that we posed no threat, the musk-ox turned its head and ambled off.

Even on days when we did not see any animals, evidence of wildlife was plentiful. Whenever we came ashore we found a network of animal tracks—the sharply pointed track of a wolf, the rounded imprint of a moose, the radial lines left by a bird claw, the chewed-up ground from a passing caribou herd. The tracks revealed an unseen drama played out by predator and prey.

We also found many bear tracks. The Horton is an important denning area for barren-ground grizzlies. We discovered several places where bears had torn open the chambers of ground squirrels in search of a meal. I never slept soundly whenever we camped near where a bear had passed.

Though thoughts of bears were disconcerting, the creature that proved to be the biggest nuisance on our trip was the lowly mosquito. Whenever we stepped on shore the insects appeared in swirling clouds, prepared to feast. To put a spoonful of food into my mouth was to swallow a garnish of the whining insects. Once when I awoke in my tent, the back of my head was swollen from bites. I saw caribou shudder and kick like wildebeests to rid themselves of the winged tormentors.

An imperturbable scientist, exposing his bare forearm to northern mosquitoes, has calculated an attack rate of 289 bites a minute. Fortunately, by applying frequent doses of repellent and wearing a mosquito-net bonnet, I was able to prevent the insects from ruining a day, and at night I could go back to wondering just how fresh those bear tracks were.

The highlight of our Horton River trip was to come at our final campsite. At last the wind subsided enough for us to move on from

Time's mute witnesses, boulders at Red Rock Coulee, in Alberta, embody the saga of ancient waters. A shallow sea covered this area some 75 million years ago, producing a thick bed of marine sediments. When the sea retreated, the sediments hardened into sandstone. Rivers later surged across the land, wearing the rock into spherical shapes. Another sea subsequently flooded the area, encasing the rocks in mud. With the erosion of this layer, rounded boulders like those below emerge. The story of the rocks continues, as freezing and thawing splits the boulders into new shapes (below, right).

where we had been forced to lay over. We traveled fast to make up time. We pitched our last camp in a tundra meadow overlooking a small delta where the Horton enters Franklin Bay, an inlet of Amundsen Gulf. From the high terrace where we camped, we could make out remnants of pack ice floating in the distance—one a beautiful blue pyramid. On the spongy ground around us grew a brilliant array of low-lying wild flowers, their miniscule blossoms red, yellow, pink, and white.

Paul and I had reached the end of the river and were now awaiting our rendezvous with the floatplane. But on the day we had arranged to be picked up, the wind slammed in from the west, bringing a dense cloud cover. The plane did not show up. On the third day of waiting, Paul was scanning the horizon when his eye caught a movement on a ridge to the west. He called out, and both of us watched in wonder as several hundred caribou came spilling down the slope onto the delta. The caribou were moving into the breeze to keep off biting mosquitoes and were unable to detect our scent. Stalled by the wind, we were now rewarded by it.

The herd, made up mostly of cows and calves, began to advance across the delta. The animals then broke into a run, surging up into the meadow where we were camped. They passed so close we could have touched their bodies. The caribou stopped and grazed on the sedge, their winter coats still shedding. They turned often to look at the pair of two-legged creatures watching them. That evening the plane appeared. When it landed on the river, we were far out on the tundra, stalking the herd for one last look.

LATER THAT SUMMER I stood on a bluff above another river, and as on the Horton I looked out over an expanse of open land. Above me I saw the same ocean of sky, and solitary falcons and hawks sailed in it. But no longer was I scanning the tundra. I was on the prairie, more than a thousand miles to the south, at the other end of Canada's interior plains. Here the land was carpeted with golden grasses. Where I stood, above the Milk River in southern Alberta—less than a day's walk from the Montana border—the grasslands dipped into an impressive canyon, one of the most scenic on the plains. Ramparts of sandstone penned in the looping Milk River. On the sites of former oxbow lakes, cottonwoods and tall grasses grew in profusion. In the distance rose Montana's Sweet Grass Hills.

I enjoyed this surprising conjunction of canyon and prairie. In his description of an 1874 Mounted Police expedition to the Milk River country, Canadian author John Peter Turner wrote: "The North-West Mounted Police had reached the inner sanctum of the untamed west. Here was a land of infinite loneliness, of sheer distance and solitude that pressed unforgettably on Eastern senses. In its utter nakedness, a world of grass and sky and mountain stood forth in magnificent perspective."

The prairie does not impress everyone, though—at least not at first. When David McIntyre took a job with the Alberta Recreation and Parks Department in its southern region, he found himself unmoved by his new surroundings. He had come from a logging job on Washington's Olympic Peninsula, where he had worked amid dense forests and towering mountains. "My first impression of the prairie was of how flat and empty it was," *(Continued on page 142)*

Alberta's Milk River curls through 500-foot-deep Milk River Canyon. Lewis and Clark discovered the river in 1805, naming it for its color, which they said "resembles tea with . . . milk." Though it meanders peacefully now, the Milk River once roared with fury. During the last ice age, glaciers blocked its northerly flow, causing it to carve a route southward. As the ice sheet receded, meltwater tore along the river's new path. The surging water sliced into the earth, shaping the present canyon. At left, a mule deer stands alert near sundown on the canyon's rubble-strewn rim.

Sacred gallery of the Plains Indians, sandstone cliffs at Writing-on-Stone Provincial Park (below) reveal one of the largest displays of Indian rock carving to be found anywhere on the North American plains. Designs include shield-bearing warriors apparently engaged in hand-to-hand combat (bottom, right). Archaeologists believe the Shoshone cut these scenes into the stone sometime before 1750. The perfect circles of some shields indicate that the artist may have used a simple pin-and-thong compass. The Indians probably carved the designs to summon guardian spirits, to record visions, and to commemorate exploits of war. A cliff face in Writing-On-Stone (right) suggests a human profile, perhaps fueling the Indians' belief that spirits inhabited the area. Uncurling from beneath a rock, a prairie rattlesnake (bottom, left) adds a sinuous line to the jagged terrain.

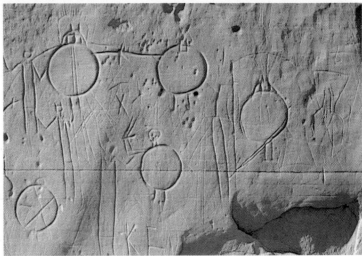

Lightning-sparked flames crackle through a forest in drought-plagued Wood Buffalo National Park. Such fires burned almost 2,500 square miles of parkland here in 1981. Located in northern Alberta and the southern Northwest Territories, Wood Buffalo provides a habitat for some 6,000 bison, the world's largest free-roaming herd. Driven by fire and smoke, a lone bull retreats to a bank of the Peace River (below), then swims a quarter of a mile to safety on the other side (bottom). Canada established Wood Buffalo—the nation's largest park—in 1922 to preserve the last herd of wood bison. The later introduction of plains bison into the park led to extensive interbreeding. In 1957 officials discovered an isolated herd of wood bison and moved the animals to new reserves to protect the strain.

Islands of spruce spring from salt flats in Wood Buffalo National Park. Remote and little-visited, Wood Buffalo contains the only natural breeding ground of the endangered whooping crane. Some 70 of the gangly white wading birds summer in marshy areas of the park. At right, a tendriled tributary runs into the Rivière des Rochers, which along with the Peace and other rivers flows into one of the world's largest inland deltas. Located on the eastern border of Wood Buffalo at the outlet of Lake Athabasca, the Peace-Athabasca Delta sits astride portions of the four major North American flyways;

each spring and fall, more than a million migrating waterfowl feed and rest here. Runoff from one of Wood Buffalo's many saline springs cakes the ground with salt (right, bottom). Indians, explorers, and early settlers collected supplies of the vital mineral in this area.

he remembered, as we drove between fields blue with the flowers of flax. "Whenever I drove across the prairie, I saw nothing between me and my destination. If you're in the mountains and you see a hawk in a clearing, you say, 'Wow!' because it seems so close. In the prairie the hawk is just a speck. The backdrop is so big it swallows everything." After several field trips, however, Dave began to pick out details within the vast, open land. "It takes a while to appreciate," he admitted. "The prairie requires a very close look."

Grooming itself during the summer rutting season, a wood bison roils the dust in a wallow at Elk Island National Park, in Alberta. Some 170,000 wood bison once roamed the boreal forests of the interior plains. Fewer than a thousand of the animals remain today.

Dave, a blond, gregarious fellow, accompanied me on a hike one day in Writing-On-Stone Provincial Park, a stretch of land in the Milk River Valley where Indians have left numerous rock carvings. Late in the afternoon we forded the Milk River at a shallow point, the cold, cloudy water pushing hard against our legs. We climbed the bank and before us unfolded the prairie, its spear grass tinted gold by the low sun.

Within minutes, Dave's sharpened vision brought the countryside to life. He pointed out a marsh hawk, recognizable from the white markings on its tail, as it hung above the ground, perhaps spying for a field mouse or a meadow vole to take back to its young. From the rim of a gully Dave sighted a mule deer and its fawn moving in the brush below. Descending into the gully, we twice disturbed prairie rattlesnakes that were sunning themselves. Each time the snake backed into shadow and coiled, rattling its tail menacingly.

Dave spotted two abandoned goose eggs on top of a hoodoo, a mushroom-shaped pinnacle of rock. We crossed the stream at the bottom of the gully by using a beaver dam as a bridge. During the ascent of the other side we flushed three great horned owls, which in another hour would be hunting. A white-tailed deer sprinted from behind a rock. I heard a series of muffled roars, and Dave gestured toward some nighthawks that were producing miniature sonic booms as they pulled out of their steep dives. A prairie falcon alighted on the ground. Dave pointed to another owl. What we both could see was that this "barren country" was crowded with life.

Virgin prairie, which once mantled all of the Great Plains, survives only in remnants now. Less intimidating than forests or mountains, its soil fertile, its grasses nutritious, its spaces largely unbroken, the prairie has always presented an exceedingly vulnerable form of wilderness. Where it still exists, it usually amounts to a small interruption in the spread of farms and towns. I could have walked from the rim of the Milk River Canyon and, within a couple of hours, come into sight of grazing cattle and dust plumes from pickup trucks. The few extensive tracts of ungrazed prairie that remain in Canada exist because of their remoteness. Most have no formal protection.

In an effort to preserve a specimen of wild prairie, the Canadian government has designated a 350-square-mile tract in southern Saskatchewan to become the country's first grasslands national park. The government has embarked on a land acquisition program in the Val Marie-Killdeer region—about 150 miles east of the Milk River Canyon—and hopes by 1988 to have a 100-square-mile section of virgin grassland ready to open to the public.

DURING THE SUMMER I made a second survey of the southern prairie region, but this time I was not looking for living creatures. I was searching for bones—clues to life in the area some 75 million years before. I had come to Dinosaur Provincial Park, 15,000 acres of badlands along the Red Deer River in southeastern Alberta. Here, amid a spectacular terrain of gullies and ridges, exists one of the most extensive dinosaur fossil beds in the world.

The park was established in 1955 to protect the fossils and landforms. Restricted access further protects some 80 percent of the park. In this area scientific researchers scour the rocks in search of prehistoric bones. To look for fossils here is to mine a mother lode. The collection rate is prodigious, as each year erosion exposes yet more bones. Since the late 1800s, when paleontologists first began excavating the Red Deer River area for fossils, more than 300 high-quality specimens have been removed from Dinosaur.

Many of the world's major natural history museums display dinosaur skeletons from these beds. Altogether, more than 30 species of dinosaurs have been identified as a result of excavations in the park. One recent important find was a limb bone of a flying reptile that indicated a possible wingspan of 45 feet. In recognition of the park's "outstanding universal significance," Dinosaur was named a world heritage site by the United Nations in 1979.

One July morning, before the summer heat had turned the badlands into a furnace, I joined Dr. Philip Currie, assistant director of research at the Tyrrell Museum of Paleontology, as he and a team of assistants scouted for bones in Dinosaur Park. Inching around narrow ledges and scrambling up and down slopes of crumbling rock made it hard at times for me to picture a moist, swampy floodplain on the edge of an interior sea. But such was the terrain, scientists theorize, when dinosaurs lived here 72 to 80 million years ago, during the age known as the late Cretaceous.

The reptiles living then included such creatures as *Centrosaurus*, a powerful rhinoceros-like creature with a horn up to a foot and a half long; *Corythosaurus*, a duckbilled giant with webbed fingers, a large helmetlike crest, and as many as 2,000 teeth; and the vicious *Dromaeosaurus*, a man-size flesh eater with a claw on the back of each foot for disemboweling its prey.

When the dinosaurs died, river sediments gradually buried

their remains, and in time both the remains and the sediments turned to rock. More sediments were laid down over millions of years, only to be eroded away by wind and water. The massive ice sheets that later crept down over Canada during the ice ages deposited vast quantities of soil on the plains. After the ice sheets retreated, wind and water erosion picked up their work again, gnarling the landscape into its present state and exposing the Cretaceous strata once more.

"Call out if you see anything," Phil Currie instructed his crew before they dispersed with hammers and awls. Of course, "anything" doesn't quite mean just anything in Dinosaur Park. Within half an hour Phil and I detected an interesting sand-colored bone protruding from the rock. After chipping around the spot, Phil, a lanky fellow in T-shirt and shorts, determined that three vertebrae were lodged in the rock. With that he walked on.

"People in other parts of the world would be excited to find that," he said over his shoulder, "but bones are so abundant here, we have to start setting priorities."

In only a few hours we could have collected dozens of fossil bone fragments, as easily as picking up pretty shells on a beach. None of the bones we saw were keepers, though. A significant find, according to Phil, would be a complete skeleton—several are found each year in the park—or a bone bed, a large concentration of bones from many animals. Bone beds resulted when ancient rivers swept up the skeletons of these animals and deposited them in pieces on the bottoms of the watercourses.

Phil is currently more interested in discovering bone beds than full skeletons. As we maneuvered up a ridge, Phil said, "When paleontologists were after skeletons, bone beds were ignored. But the science of paleontology has developed significantly from bone beds. They provide much more information than isolated skeletons do,

such as the faunal mix of an area or its population density." On this day we came across no bone beds. One assistant did find the lower jaw of a crocodilian and another located an eight-inch-long dinosaur toe bone. But the day did not discourage the leader.

Speaking with the relish of an antique collector who knows he has found a worthy attic, Phil reported that, "In one half section [320 acres] we found 50 bone beds last year." He paused, then added, "And there are 15,000 acres in the park."

Sometimes, the fossil hunters in Dinosaur Park pick up an arrowhead or a piece of stone that has been worked, evidence of the Indians who once dwelled on the prairie. Indians first came to the grasslands more than 5,000 years ago, following the herds of bison and settling in or near the river valleys. Scores of tepee rings can be seen from the air above the northern rim of the Milk River Canyon. By the end of the 19th century, the Indian tribes of this region—the Blackfoot, Cree, Gros Ventre, Shoshone, and Assiniboin—had been driven from much of their prairie homeland by the white man.

Unlike the prairie tribes, the Indians that live in the vast, thinly populated boreal forest to the north remain relatively isolated even today. In August, I joined Paul von Baich in Yellowknife, capital of the Northwest Territories. There we chartered a floatplane to take us a hundred miles northwest to the Indian village of Lac la Martre, accessible by road only in the winter, when snow provides a surface firm enough to support vehicles. We were traveling to Lac la Martre on the advice of Roman Catholic missionary René Fumoleau, an author and filmmaker who has lived with the native people of the north for nearly 30 years. Father Fumoleau had told us we would be able to see Indians at Lac la Martre who carry on wilderness activities in the manner of their ancestors.

As we flew over the now familiar terrain of the northern plains—made up of seemingly equal (Continued on page 150)

Lowering clouds scud above the Indian village of Lac la Martre, in the Northwest Territories. The 260 Dogrib Indians of Lac la Martre rely heavily on fishing as a food source. During the warm months, villagers tend fishnets on the adjacent lake in their brightly painted boats. In winter, the men hunt caribou, dividing the meat among members of the community. Many of the villagers spend about six months a year trapping for fur. Though the people follow such traditional activities, their 200-year-old settlement displays telltale signs of the modern world: Power lines knit the sturdy log houses of Lac la Martre. The pace of change here promises to pick up. In 1981 the villagers voted to bring television and telephones to their homes.

Placid waters of Lac la Martre capture evening's fiery show. Though remote, the lake bears signs

of man's long habitation: Old fishing camps and trappers' cabins dot the wooded shoreline.

Channels and lakes etch a quicksilver tracery in a section of the Mackenzie River Delta (right). At a fishing camp along the Mackenzie, Vitaline Manuel (above), a Hare Indian, prepares for winter by hanging whitefish to dry in the sun. The camp lies below sheer limestone walls known as the Ramparts (left). Native people have used this site for centuries. Some 25,000 years ago, the Mackenzie Valley may have served as an ice-free migration route used by Indians to reach central North America. Today's Mackenzie Valley tribes seek political and cultural autonomy through negotiations with the federal government.

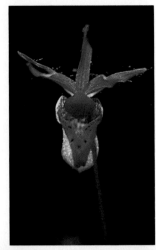

Summer is a many-petaled thing in Cypress Hills Provincial Park, in southern Alberta. A slipper-like blossom distinguishes the fairy slipper (top), one of 14 kinds of orchids that grow in the area. The bright flowers of the buffalo bean (center) give way to poisonous seeds. Herald of spring, the pasqueflower (bottom) often pushes up through snow to blossom.

parts of forest and water—I recalled the words of Father Fumoleau, who earlier in the day had informed us: "There is no word in the Indian language up here for wilderness. There is no wilderness. It is all home to them."

We soon spotted the village below us, cut from the forest on the southeastern corner of Lac la Martre. We landed and taxied across the lake to a pier at the village, where we were greeted by a group of chattering, dark-haired Indian children. After unloading our gear, we walked into the village. Most of the houses were well-constructed log cabins. Next to many of them stood poles arranged in the shape of tepee frames, from which hung splayed fish being dried. On the cabin roofs we saw such objects as boat frames, moose antlers, dogsleds, and fishnets. Dogs tied to stakes behind the houses barked and wailed as we passed.

The 260 residents of Lac la Martre, with the exception of the co-op manager and two schoolteachers, are members of the Dogrib tribe, one of several Athapaskan-speaking tribes that inhabit most of the forested regions of northern Canada. Paul and I were taken to see Chief Johnny Nitsiza. A middle-aged man with a deeply lined face, he greeted us from his bed, where he was resting under a brightly colored religious wall hanging.

Speaking through an interpreter, the chief informed us that winter is the busiest time for his people, when some 10 to 15 families, about half the village, set up traplines and establish camps in the bush. "In February we have the caribou hunt," Chief Nitsiza said. "Each household sends a man, and whatever meat is taken is divided among members of the community. The hunt used to be in August. We chartered planes to take us to the caribou grounds, but it became too expensive. Now we go hunting during the winter . . . and take snowmobiles."

For three days Paul and I stayed in the village. One day we stopped by a cabin where a mother and her son were sitting on the floor around a wood-burning stove. They were cutting up the carcasses of a moose and a bear, which the woman's husband had shot the day before. "We want to use the meat for a village feast," the woman said as she stood up and dropped a large dark-brown moose liver into a pot of boiling water.

Paul and I also saw a few less traditional activities, such as a Sunday prayer meeting and a game of baseball. For the baseball game, the boys used a bat carved from a spruce limb. The players wore caps that assigned them to teams from distant villages, such as Pittsburgh and Boston.

During the first part of our visit we sometimes grew restless because of the slow pace of village life; the time reminded us of our windbound days on the Horton River. But gradually our perspective shifted as we found ourselves adapting to the tempo of the village. We realized that the quiet rhythm of these days must come close to what life had been like all over northern Canada before the white man arrived. At Lac la Martre, the villagers hunt, fish, and trap according to the prescribed seasons. In between these tasks the people mostly relax in their homes, talking to family or friends and sometimes tanning hides or preparing fish to dry. The villagers know their next outing for food will come soon enough.

Another floatplane landed on the lake during our stay and, as always, several villagers wandered down to the pier. In the plane was the village's council chairman, Isadore Zoe, who was returning from Yellowknife, where he had been briefed on the latest political developments affecting the village. The Dogribs, together with the other tribes of the Mackenzie River Valley—the Kutchin, Slave, Chipewyan, and Hare—formed a political brotherhood in 1970, later named the Dene Nation. Dene is the Athapaskan word for "the people." In the summer of 1981, the Dene, along with the Metis Association, which represents Canadians of mixed blood, entered into negotiations with the federal government over the right to establish a self-governing province. Included in the negotiations is a land claim for 650,000 square miles of land in the Mackenzie Valley.

"We're not just talking about an area of land," I was told by Dene President Georges Erasmus. "The land could even be a minor point. What is important to us is the right to have enough authority and power to flourish as a culture and a people." The Dene recently exerted enough power to persuade the government to delay construction of an oil pipeline in the southern Mackenzie Valley until their land claims are discussed in further detail. Some Canadians fear, however, that the Dene Nation will want to secede from Canada. Georges Erasmus disagrees. "This is definitely not a separatist movement," he stressed. "The basis of our nation is culture, and we want to enter into the Canadian Confederation on that basis."

Regardless of the outcome of the Dene Nation's negotiations, it is certain that the village of Lac la Martre faces change. Plans call for the government to bring telephones and television to the village. We glimpsed how these modern conveniences may alter village life in a story told to us one night by Alexander Nitsiza, secretary of Lac la Martre's village council.

Alex mentioned that a bear had attacked his house recently. "It was late fall and this thin, hungry black bear was prowling around the house. Pretty soon it started scratching on the door, trying to break in. I got worried, so I went to get my rifle, but I found that I had no ammunition. Lucky for me the door was strong, and after a while the bear ran away." Alex paused, then suddenly brightened, adding, "If that happens after we get telephones, I'll pick up the phone and *call* someone to come over with a gun."

MY FINAL STOP in the interior plains was at Wood Buffalo National Park, a huge spread of wilderness that straddles the border between Alberta and the Northwest Territories, just south of Great Slave Lake. At 17,300 square miles—about four-fifths the size of Nova Scotia—Wood Buffalo is the largest park in Canada, and among the largest in the world. Its terrain is primarily a mélange of bogs, slow-running streams, wide rivers, and shallow lakes interspersed with meadowland and forests of spruce, pine, and aspen.

Wood Buffalo was established in 1922 to protect Canada's last remaining herd of wood bison, a larger and darker relative of the plains bison. Later, from 1925 to 1928, the government transferred nearly 7,000 plains bison to the park. The unintended result was an interbreeding with the 1,500 wood bison already there.

For years, the interbreeding was thought to have extinguished the pure strain of wood bison. But an aerial survey in 1957 detected a small, isolated herd of wood bison, which officials relocated to

Bulbous heads bowed, prairie smoke (below) blooms with a spiky exuberance. Indians sometimes brew tea from the plant's roots. Colorful shooting stars (bottom) point earthward like plummeting meteors.

Elk Island National Park, in Alberta, and to a preserve bordering Great Slave Lake. The current Wood Buffalo herd of roughly 6,000 animals—all thought to be hybrids—is the largest free-roaming bison herd in the world. The creatures retain the dusky appearance and larger girth of the wood bison, and, it also appears, their nimble footing among the trees. One day I saw a group of about 15 bison. It was rutting season, and I could see two large, bearded suitors jostling for position next to a cow. I was surprised to see bison in a forest, having always observed them before on the prairie.

When I approached them, the bison quickly retreated a few feet into the forest, behind a row of aspen. The 2,000-pound animals peered out at me as if confident they were hiding their bulks behind the thin trees. When I took another step, the bison vanished into the forest with a stealth I could scarcely have imagined.

The park's other famous tenant is the endangered whooping crane. In 1954 forestry service personnel discovered the only natural breeding site of these long-legged waders. Each spring the whoopers return to the northeast corner of Wood Buffalo after having wintered in the Aransas National Wildlife Refuge, on the Texas coast.

Despite the fame of the whoopers, it is rare that a park visitor will see one of the large white birds. Park officials zealously protect their nesting site from the curious. Currently about 70 whooping cranes spend the warm months in the park. Unfortunately, 1981 proved to be a disastrous year for the cranes. Because of dry conditions, predators were able to reach many of the birds' nests, which are normally protected by surrounding water. Only three young whoopers survived from the nesting, one of which later died when it struck a power line during the flock's migration south.

Wood Buffalo is bordered on the east by the Slave and Athabasca Rivers, waterways once traveled by fur traders and explorers. Near the southeast corner of the park is the Peace-Athabasca Delta, one of the world's largest inland deltas. It forms where the Peace, Athabasca, and Birch Rivers deposit their sediments at the outlet of Lake Athabasca. In spring and fall, the food-rich delta abounds with waterfowl. More than a million geese, swans, and ducks from four North American flyways visit here on their lengthy migrations.

Along the eastern side of the park, on the Slave River, is another sort of boundary, one that has stood for millions of years. Here amid booming rapids, islands of reddish granite jut from the water. These outcroppings represent the dividing line between the Canadian Shield and the interior plains, as bold a division in its way as the high mountains are in the west.

Surprisingly, Wood Buffalo is relatively unknown, despite the superlative nature of its wilderness. Distant from cities and superhighways, its facilities limited to one campground, and its trails made mostly by game, the park does not attract casual visitors. Its visitor count, excluding people who come from nearby towns, totals between 500 and 800 a year. In high season, as many people as that pass through Banff National Park, in the Canadian Rockies, in less than a day.

The irony of Wood Buffalo is that a wilderness so enormous, so remote, and so little-visited could be besieged by pressures from the outside world. Yet that is precisely the case, for the park is tied to the past. Under existing game regulations, up to 370 native people a

Battle regalia: Head net and long sleeves protect the author against the onslaught of the north's tiny furies—mosquitoes (top). Although mosquitoes feed on flower nectar, females require a meal of blood to produce eggs. Above, a mosquito lands on an Indian paintbrush. Northerners have resorted to desperate measures to ward off the swarming insects, including smearing their bodies with lard and sitting in campfire smoke.

year are allowed to take out licenses to hunt or to trap in the park. Cree Indians have recently established a community inside the park in anticipation of a land claim settlement stemming from a 19th-century treaty. And a timber company is harvesting magnificent stands of white spruce along the Peace River under terms of a lease signed 30 years ago, when Wood Buffalo was administered outside the national parks system.

Modernity besets the park as well. Bennett Dam, constructed in neighboring British Columbia at a site nearly 700 miles upriver from Lake Athabasca, regulates up to 50 percent of the Peace River's flow. Controlling the river's natural flow has interrupted the cyclical flooding that is necessary for the delta marshland to restore itself. And another dam is being considered near the park boundary on the Slave River rapids. In addition, the territorial government and the business community in Fort Smith, site of the park headquarters, are pushing for a new road through Wood Buffalo. Park officials fear that the increased traffic the new road would bring might disrupt the wildlife.

For reasons such as these, the administrators of Wood Buffalo face a difficult task in balancing contending interests. "There are just too many pressures," Superintendent Bernie Lieff told me. "I'll guarantee you that in ten years the park boundaries will not be the same." To cope with circumstances, officials at Wood Buffalo are preparing a 15-year management plan that they believe will serve as a model for any future park where the wilderness must exist within a thicket of commercial, political, and cultural demands.

In spite of its administrative entanglements, Wood Buffalo offers a rich experience to those who enter its wilderness. While in the park, I took a backpack trip with park employees Michael Cobus and Mary Jean Bossenmaier and local outfitter Jacques van Pelt. More than 20 fires, all lightning-caused, were raging within the park boundaries at the time, thickening the air with smoke and closing most of the park to visitors. The fires would take an eventual toll of some 2,450 square miles of parkland.

After picking a smoke-free part of the park, Michael, Mary Jean, Jacques, and I set out through a dense forest of jack pine. We were following a wide bison path. "We will go at the rhythm of the animals," Jacques said as we stepped over fallen trees and skirted ponds. We climbed down a steep slope to a gleaming salt flat, stopping at one of the saline springs to cool ourselves in the icy water. In the distance stood islands of tall spruce, and on the ground grew fiery red patches of the salt-resistant plant, samphire.

As I looked out over yet another wilderness vista, I realized that during my travels in the interior plains I had rarely proclaimed the region's beauty. The land had seemed too stark, too challenging, too boundless for such an appraisal. The wilderness had simply not allowed for much spectatorship. It had enveloped me with its rain and wind, its rocks and ridges, its heat and cold.

I knew now that those thrilling sights the wilderness bestows —a pair of wolf cubs standing silently on a shore, a hawk soaring overhead, the sun painting the walls of a canyon—were never to be taken for granted. They came at their own pace and of their own calling. And in my short time in this spacious land, I discovered a deep pleasure in obeying those age-old rhythms.

Wending north toward the Arctic Ocean, the Horton River loops through a quiet valley just below the tree line. Encountered in 1826 by members of a British expedition searching for the Northwest Passage, the Horton awaited exploration for nearly a hundred years. Even today, few people travel on the remote river. The only sign of man seen by the author and the photographer during a two-week canoe trip: an old ax mark on a tree beside the river. A caribou bull (above), part of the Bluenose herd, crosses a gravel bar along the Horton, taking advantage of breezes that help keep away insects.

Wispy layers of mist envelop the emerald hills of the Horton River Valley. In this pristine wilderness

setting, barren-ground grizzly bears, peregrine falcons, and other animals live unmolested.

Western Canada

By Ron Fisher • Photographs by Sam Abell

Dall's sheep find lush summer grasses on an alpine slope in Kluane National Park. Kluane lies deep within the massive, glacier-veined St. Elias Mountains, part of western Canada's vast cordillera.

ARCTIC OCEAN

Beaufort Sea

ALASKA

Porcupine

Old Crow

Arctic Coastal Plain

Firth

Tree Line

ARCTIC CIRCLE

Richardson Mountains

UNITED STATES
CANADA

Dawson

YUKON
TERRITORY

Yukon

KLUANE
NATIONAL PARK

Mount Logan +

St. Elias Mountains

Haines
Junction

★ Whitehorse

Two major ranges and many smaller mountain chains wrinkle western Canada from the U.S.-Canadian border to the northern Yukon Territory. Along the west coast, storms lash the rain forests of Vancouver Island and the Queen Charlotte Islands. Eastward, the Coast Mountains create an arid zone in their lee. Farther east, pine trees cloak lake-studded valleys in the province of Alberta. In northern British Columbia, the mountain ranges form rugged parklands. Glaciers slide from enormous ice fields in the southwestern Yukon, and in the far north the mountains subside into the tundra of the Arctic Coastal Plain.

Juneau ★

Telegraph
Creek

Stikine

+ *Mount Edziza*

MOUNT EDZIZA
PROVINCIAL PARK

SPATSIZI PLATEAU
WILDERNESS PARK

R O C K Y   M O U N T A I N S

ALBERTA

★ Edmonton

Prince Rupert

BRITISH
COLUMBIA

*Queen Charlotte
Islands*

Hecate Strait

C O A S T   M O U N T A I N S

Fraser

Chilcotin

JASPER
NATIONAL PARK

WHITE GOAT
WILDERNESS AREA

Big Creek

*Chilko
Lake*

Fraser

BANFF
NATIONAL PARK

Calgary

PACIFIC OCEAN

*Vancouver
Island*

Vancouver

CANADA
UNITED STATES

0 KILOMETERS   400

0 STATUTE MILES   200

PACIFIC RIM
NATIONAL PARK

Victoria ★

I'm lying on my stomach, watching a mountain goat. The goat is lying on *its* stomach, watching me. My elbows and knees are grinding painfully into a bed of sharp gravel, but the goat looks comfortable. By arching my neck, I can just see him, some 30 yards away, over a rocky ridge. The goat has tucked his legs under him, like a cat. He's in a sunny spot on a bed of late-summer grass in Mount Edziza Provincial Park, in northern British Columbia.

Western Canada

The goat endured my presence for half an hour, then stood up. He stretched, wriggled his ears, then stood staring at the ground. The fur on his legs came down only to his ankles, like a man whose trousers are too short: You could see his socks. He was pure white, with black, soulful eyes, backward curving black horns, and a big black nose. He turned his back and walked slowly away, pausing once in a while to look over his shoulder at me. Now and then he flapped an ear. He disappeared slowly onto the face of a cliff below me, on a path only a goat could see and only a goat could follow.

The wall he descended was one side of a ravine several hundred feet deep and a mile or so wide. The ravine had been carved by a nameless stream on its way to join Mess Creek. After winding northward for a few miles, Mess Creek joins the Stikine River. The Stikine, in turn, flows westward through the Coast Mountains, crosses a narrow strip of Alaska, and empties into the Pacific Ocean. The Stikine watershed covers 20,000 square miles, about 5 percent of British Columbia. The goat and I were in the heart of an immense wilderness.

I had come to Mount Edziza with photographer Sam Abell. Together, we would spend a summer exploring western Canada: the coast, the tundra, and the cordillera—the chains of mountains that stretch from the U. S.-Canadian border far into the Yukon Territory. We were to discover a wildly varied land. The rain-drenched coast nurtures lush forests where the moss grows thick. In the mountains, glaciers grumble and slide, slowly undoing the mountain-building work of millennia. In the plateau region between the two great western mountain systems—the Rockies and the Coast Mountains—prickly pears cower beneath a blazing sun, and cattle nibble dry grasses in the shade of lodgepole pine forests. Far to the north, the tundra, spongy as a mattress, edges the Arctic Ocean.

The west coast of Canada wriggles and squirms to such an extent that, in its 550-mile length, there are several thousand miles of coastline. Here are the country's tallest trees and lushest vegetation. Set off from the rest of mainland Canada by the barrier of the Coast Mountains, the west coast forms a sort of cage. The mountains keep some species of plants and animals in, and others out. Sitka spruce, for instance, appear only on the west coast, while white spruce and black spruce grow throughout the rest of Canada.

It's a narrow strip, this coastal region, barely a few days' hike across. Given the inclination, a trekker could move inland from a zone of tides and seashore, up through dripping rain forests to subalpine forest, on up to alpine meadows, and arrive at the top to stroll across the arctic-type tundra of the Coast Mountains.

Sam and I began our summer in Canada in this coastal zone—on Vancouver Island. We drove one day from Victoria to Tofino, on the Pacific side of the island, through mountains and forests. Here mist turns to rain, then back to mist. Clouds drip wisps of fog into

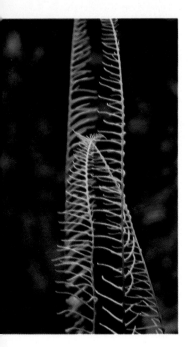

Young deer fern on Vancouver Island unfurls tender fiddlehead fronds. Several kinds of plants and animals live only along Canada's western coast, trapped behind the barrier of the Coast Mountains. Among the animals found nowhere else in Canada: the northwestern crow, the mountain beaver, and the black-tailed deer.

Common on the west coast of Vancouver Island, dwarf dogwood (opposite, top) provides cover and food for a giant Pacific slug (opposite, lower). Also called bunchberry, dwarf dogwood thrives in many parts of North America, from Alaska to Maryland.

valleys, and peaks puncture the clouds. The mountains act as a giant fist, squeezing rain from the spongelike clouds that sail in from the Pacific. Trickles of water tumble down the slopes and turn into gushes, which turn into rivers, which become lakes.

Long Beach, a unit of Pacific Rim National Park, runs down the west coast of Vancouver Island for 15 miles. We walked it one drizzly day in the company of Jim Darling, a young Canadian who has spent several summers on the island working for the park and studying whales. He talked of gray whales migrating: "About 16,000 whales go by Long Beach every year, and you can sit out on a rock and watch them, practically reach out and touch them. Frankly, they don't always look as if they know exactly what they're doing; they seem to navigate by bumping from rock to rock, and some appear to get lost in the inlets, but they manage to find their way out."

At Radar Hill, site of a World War II radar installation, we descended to the beach on a steep and muddy forest slope. A winter wren sang somewhere in the treetops, piping us downward. Waves pushed against the shore with relentless vigor. Gulls fluttered and bathed in the backwash, and clouds of mist, born of the cracking surf, drifted inland toward the forest. Bald eagles soared overhead.

Around the rocky points, heaps of jagged boulders made the going slow and tricky. In the intertidal zone, masses of shiny starfish—in oranges, purples, and browns—clung together on wet boulders. Mussels and barnacles coated the rocks. Leaning close, you could hear the faint rustling clatter of their bizarre society. Anemones waited in tide pools. Doughnut-shaped, frilly creatures, they can enfold themselves around a mussel, digest its flesh, then spit out the shell. In the surging waves, harbor seals peeked out of the water with whiskered, doggy faces.

On another drizzly day I walked in the rain forest, just inland from the beach. It was quiet, with only the sound of water running and dripping and pattering on my poncho hood, and sudden bird cries in the trees high overhead. My breath came in visible, humid puffs, even on this warm summer afternoon. Leaves dripped droplets into quiet puddles of reflected trees.

As I stood quietly, surrounded by trees with trunks as wide as my office, a hummingbird came and hovered by my ear; we startled each other, and I jumped. Beside me, a pale two-inch-long slug sat on a broad leaf, nearly half of which it had eaten. It seemed a shortsighted policy, like sawing off a limb you're sitting on. Saucer-like cobwebs, almost too delicate to see, bridged gaps in the shrubs. As I leaned forward to examine one, I put my face through another and caused a flurry of rebuilding by a BB-size spider.

There was a smell of growth and decay, and giant ferns grew at the edge of the trail. Cobwebby fingers of moss hung from the limbs and branches. Toppled trees waved tangles of exposed, moss-covered roots, like feet kicking in the air. Fallen spruce and hemlock logs take a century to rot here. It's been said that the trees are never so alive as when they're dead: A host of plants and animals go to work on them immediately, eventually reducing them to soil.

Forests cover about 55 percent of British Columbia. The trees—especially the Douglas fir, Sitka spruce, western hemlock, and western red cedar—mean more than beauty. All summer long I would find that where there are trees in western Canada, there are loggers. And where there are loggers, there are groups, clubs, and citizen associations trying either to stop them or to move them somewhere else.

Up the coast 140 miles from Vancouver Island, in the Queen Charlotte Islands, I was given a pessimistic prognosis for the forests there by charter boat skipper Art Babcock. "If there's something here you'd like to see, you'd better see it now, because in ten years it'll be gone." All around us were mountains that had been clear-cut—as closely shaved as the heads of Marine Corps recruits.

Sam and I spent eight days with Art and his wife, Annie, cruising the 150 or so islands of the Queen Charlotte group. The Charlottes, about 4,000 square miles of land, are formed around a backbone of the same mountain chain that rises on Vancouver Island; the mountains dip beneath the sea to reappear here. Turbulent Hecate Strait, up to 80 miles wide, separates the Charlottes from the mainland.

Aboard the 45-foot M. V. *Bajo Point*, a trawler converted for charter and painted a fetching forest green, we headed south from Queen Charlotte City. The day was calm and sunny, a rarity for the rainy and storm-battered Charlottes. We would eat and sleep aboard the boat, and use a 14-foot inflatable raft with a powerful outboard motor for exploring the shores of the islands.

Also aboard was Keith Hodson, a former field worker with British Columbia's fish and wildlife agency who had quit government work to become a farmer in the central part of the province. Keith's first love—almost an obsession—is a species of bird found on many sheer cliff faces in the Charlottes, the peregrine falcon.

"When my brother and I got out of high school, we bought an old wood-and-canvas canoe and took it up into northern British Columbia," Keith said. "We spent six weeks in that canoe and ended up in the Arctic Ocean. We counted pairs of peregrine falcons along the way, and that was the beginning of my interest in wildlife."

Whenever we went ashore in the raft, Keith kept a careful watch for falcons. At cliff faces he would idle the engine and clap his hands sharply to startle them into flight. Nesting season was over, and he could distinguish the juveniles from the adults. "Young ones are a little darker and fly a little . . . floppier," he said.

In 1774, when the Spanish explorer Juan Perez anchored his corvette *Santiago* off the northern end of the Charlottes—the first European to visit them—he found villages of Haida Indians. The Haida were scattered throughout the islands. Today about 1,600 Haida still live on the Charlottes, owning and manning many of the fishing boats that work in the surrounding waters.

The modern Haida have created a powerful native art movement that is producing a school of accomplished carvers. They have a noble tradition upon which to draw. The remarkable Haida totem poles—fantastic figures of ravens, eagles, bears, and frogs, all seemingly devouring one another—dumbfounded the early European explorers and, though some totem poles have been collected by museums, others still stand in the wild where they were erected.

At Anthony Island, a little clump of rock near the southernmost tip of the Charlottes (and the island for which Keith named his third son), the Haida built some of their finest totems. A few still stand, or rather lean, gradually succumbing to mold and rot.

"It's been said that there is strength in the totem poles," Annie Babcock told me, "even the toppled and decaying ones, because strong thought went into them." The totems often represented family lineages and sometimes mythical figures or events.

A little doe, very tame, wandered among the poles. There was a patter of rain on my tent in the night. The ancient Haida, with a nod to their wretched weather, wove broadbrim rain hats for themselves from roots and bark. I emerged in the morning into a sodden, dripping world of ooze and growth. Fog hid the nearby islands, and the wind made the forest moan.

Windy Bay, on Lyell Island, may be the prettiest spot in the Charlottes. It is also one of the last remaining undisturbed ecosystems of its kind in Canada. A little stream winds through the rain forest here, crosses a meadow, and empties into Hecate Strait. Windy Bay is the sort of place where, as you walk along the creek, you find yourself whispering, and the phrase "carpet of moss" seems not to be a cliché. Moss covers everything—fallen logs, stumps, the ground, boulders—with an astonishing green blanket. There are 12-foot-thick trees here that were growing before Columbus landed in the New World.

As we chugged into the bay, I counted, in five minutes: six bald eagles; two harbor seals eyeing us from the water; a squadron of color-splashed harlequin ducks skimming across the bay; several oyster catchers, black birds with gaudy orange bills; an ancient murrelet, prime prey of peregrines, swimming with a watchful look; and two deer, stepping daintily across the meadow. There were perhaps a dozen eagles in all in the area, and we stood on the stream bank and watched as they came whistling through the trees, following the curving course of the stream. It was so still you could hear the beating of their wings and see the glitter in their black, glassy eyes.

There is an effort afoot by local citizens to persuade the provincial government to designate Windy Bay an ecological reserve, similar to a U. S. wilderness area. Windy Bay will be lucky to make it. Its only designation to date is "Block #3, Tree Farm Licence #24": It is scheduled to be clear-cut in the '80s. As we left Windy Bay, Art— who has worked as a logger—said simply and with finality: "There are some places that should not be logged, and there are some ways logging should not be done."

BACK ON THE MAINLAND, Sam and I followed the Pacific clouds eastward across the Coast Mountains to a different climate and terrain. To the east of the mountains is an area climatologists call a rain shadow. Precipitation here decreases dramatically from that west of the mountains—from as much as 300 inches a year on parts of the coast to something like 10 to 30 inches a year in the heart of the rain shadow, in the Chilcotin area. This is cattle country, reminiscent of the southwestern U. S. Low rolling hills are covered with bunchgrass, bitterroot, and scruffy lodgepole pine forests.

Chilko Lake is a good place to see the transition from the well-watered coast to the drier rain shadow. One end of the 40-mile-long lake lies in the Coast Mountains among snowcapped peaks and glaciers. But float from the lake on the Chilko River, where the spring salmon flit like red torpedoes, and you see the countryside changing. Canyons cut by the river take on the look of Utah, with sagebrush and prickly pear growing on the gravelly slopes. Ravens wheel overhead in the heated, quiet air, and goats clatter along rocky canyon walls.

This is a territory for horse-packing, and I spent a few days astride Smokey Joe, bouncing inelegantly through the area around Big Creek with a group led by wrangler Monty Klassen. We descended one day down the steep slope of a canyon wall, the horses stumbling and puffing, to the Chilcotin River, an astonishing turquoise, the only swath of color in an otherwise brown landscape. The thirsty horses waded right in, buried their snouts in the cool water, and drank until sated.

At night around a roaring fire, Monty got out his guitar and sang songs of lonely men and wicked women, of movin' on and broken hearts. He paused once to say, "Gotta roll me a skinny one." He could roll a cigarette with one hand as he rode, controlling his horse and leading the packhorse with the other. When I asked him for a permanent address, Monty was hard put to come up with one, finally settling on General Delivery. He was a patient guide as he led us across the dusty, rolling hills of the rain shadow. Cattle, at a density of less than one per acre, which is all the land can support, gave us baleful stares as they stood in the shade of the pines. I awoke here one night with both frost and ashes from the fire speckling my sleeping bag. Cold stars glittered overhead. I had been awakened by a pack of coyotes moving down a draw, singing and yapping. The horses blew and stamped, then we all went back to sleep.

Coyotes howling in the night are part of a mental image of wilderness that many of us carry around in our heads. My picture also includes a lake, mountains, and tall pines. I found such a place even farther east—in Alberta, where the White Goat Wilderness Area nestles next to Banff and Jasper National Parks on the eastern edge of the Rocky Mountains. When we camped on the tree-ringed shore of Pinto Lake, just outside the wilderness area, we found half a dozen British soldiers already in residence, led by a tall, brown-haired captain, Graham Kerr. As the men stood around the fire having coffee, I talked with Captain Kerr.

"These men are all volunteers in the Adventure Training Program," he told me. "We spend two weeks in the Canadian Rockies, though there are also training centers in Germany, in the United Kingdom, and in Cyprus. The program is meant to develop the lads' endurance and fitness in a series of outdoor disciplines—rafting, canoeing, trekking, rock-climbing, ski-mountaineering. Some of it's a good deal dangerous, but the theory is this: Applying some pressure gives you insight into a bloke's character." He laughed. "I try to frighten 'em, but not kill 'em."

In the morning they planned to climb a ragged mountain nearby, the last exercise of their two weeks. After dinner, Captain Kerr gave his little command some schooling in navigation. He passed out compasses and maps and gave them problems to solve. "You're here and you want to be there. What's your compass heading?" The math gave the troops a little trouble. One, Bill, would have ended up in the right place, "but only by walking backward," according to the captain. Bill took some kidding.

They were a hearty and fit-looking (Continued on page 176)

Growth runs rampant in a rain forest inside Pacific Rim National Park, just inland from the coast of Vancouver Island. Ocean clouds, heavy with moisture, dump some 200 inches of rainfall here each year; the forest responds with dramatic lushness. Western red cedar trees may reach a diameter of 14 feet and live for 1,200 years. Beards and coats of ferns, mosses, and lichens mantle trees and shrubs. Deriving their moisture and nutrients from the rain and the air, these plants—called epiphytes—use other plants for support. A shade-tolerant undergrowth—largely huckleberry, sphagnum moss, salal, and deer fern—crowds the forest floor.

High but not dry, a tangle of starfish clings to a boulder at low tide. The starfish attach themselves firmly with tiny suction cups. Some can withstand a hundred-pound tug. Though called ocher starfish, they often assume hues of orange, purple, or brown.

Gulls and sea lions share the surf-battered shores of the Queen Charlotte Islands. At right, a herd of northern sea lion cows and bulls lolls on a rock. The glaucous-winged gulls below nest on Anthony Island, near the southern tip of the Charlottes. Hecate Strait, some 80 miles of stormy water, separates the 150 or so islands of the Queen Charlottes from the mainland. Largely uninhabited, the islands have for eons provided a haven for a rich and varied fauna: Black bears and deer prowl meadows and riverbanks; bald eagles scavenge beaches; enormous colonies of shorebirds darken barren, rocky islets; and peregrine falcons nest on sheer cliff faces. Today the growl and chatter of logging equipment echo off the islands' forested mountainsides, and citizen groups battle to halt the clear-cutting of spruce and cedar. Haida Indians, descendants of the ancient Haida who settled here, live on the larger islands and man rugged little fishing boats that cruise turbulent offshore waters for salmon.

Inexorably, death and decay recycle the works of man and nature in the lush Queen Charlotte Islands. At Skedans, once a thriving village, the forest slowly claims a Haida totem pole (opposite). The Haida carved many such poles, both to honor ancestors and to record the mythologies and histories of their families. Some totems still stand at scattered points throughout the islands; others have been transported to museums around the world. On nearby Lyell Island, decay reduces a fallen tree to a sagging skeleton (right). Haida skulls wearing caps of moss (lower) rest near an abandoned village.

Wrangler Monty Klassen leads a packhorse down erosion-scarred bluffs edging the sinuous Chilcotin River, in south-central British Columbia. In this part of western Canada the Coast Mountains create a rain shadow, a relatively dry area in the lee of a mountain range. Here prickly pear and sagebrush grow on rolling hills, and scrubby stands of lodgepole pine shade herds of tough cattle that roam the region's enormous ranches.

Playing a lively western ballad, Duane Witte, owner of the Teepee Heart Ranch, near Big Creek, entertains guests at his spread as evening falls.

Pale glacial melt threads a narrow natural causeway between two small lakes in the White Goat

Wilderness Area, one of three wilderness tracts in the Rockies of western Alberta set aside in the 1960s.

bunch, and I poked my head out of my tent the next morning to see them off. It was raining gently, and their mountain had disappeared in a cloud. It looked like a terrible morning for climbing.

With the British Army moved out, peace came to Pinto Lake. It was an idyllic spot. A duck paddled serenely across the calm lake, then suddenly disappeared, as if something had grabbed it by the legs. In a few moments it reappeared, ruffled its feathers, and resumed paddling. Kingfishers skimmed low across the lake, then abruptly hurled themselves into the water as if they'd been shot, only to emerge from the splash with tiny silver fish in their beaks. A little bird, a kind of flycatcher I think, hovered and snatched a mosquito out of the air four feet in front of my face.

I was awakened one morning by a splashing in the Cline River, which emptied from the lake right beside our campsite. A cow moose and her calf, a smaller, browner version of herself, slowly waded downstream. They stopped once in a while to look toward our tents, then resumed feeding on the plants that grew on the bottom of the shallow river. The moose exhaled with their snouts underwater, blowing bubbles.

FOLLOW THE ROCKY MOUNTAINS north far enough and you'll find they begin to crowd against smaller ranges, producing, on a physical map of British Columbia, a tangled mix of rivers, peaks, forests, tablelands, and ravines. British Columbia has established several parks here in the north, including Spatsizi Plateau Wilderness and Mount Edziza. With 2,600 square miles, Spatsizi is the second largest park in the province, topped only by Tweedsmuir farther south.

Keith Hodson, our friend from the Queen Charlotte Islands, rejoined us in Spatsizi. Keith was familiar with the park, having worked in the area in his days with the fish and wildlife agency, and also having accompanied hunters here. We camped in Spatsizi at the end of a miniature lake in a valley a mile or so wide, with mountains rising around us. The sky was clear, except for one little cloud the size of a golf ball. The severed head of a marmot nearby was a gruesome sign of bear. The day we settled in, a helicopter made

Arctic ground squirrel, hiding in a boulder sandwich, chatters indignantly in Mount Edziza Provincial Park. "When it chattered, its entire body quivered with anger," said the author.

several passes down the valley, not in itself unusual: Even in the wildest and remotest parts of western Canada, helicopters sometimes flutter overhead like alarming mechanical insects.

I sat in the sun-warmed grass and, through a spotting scope, watched roly-poly, happy-go-lucky marmots on a sunny hillside. When two noticed each other, they would approach, sniff noses, then stand on their hind legs and give each other a little hug, like two Frenchmen. They would wrestle, puppy-like, rolling over, gnawing at each other's throats, kicking and scratching. Then they'd scamper back to their burrows.

The next day I wandered down the valley and half a mile away found a camp of geologists. Howard "Tip" Tipper, a scientist with the Geological Survey of Canada, was in charge, and three students were assisting him. They were working a rich fossil bed at the edge of an anticline, an arch of stratified rock. Tip joined the Survey in 1946, he told me, and has worked in the field all over British Columbia nearly every summer since.

"My work is my vacation," he said.

One of the students was Jasmine Hobart, from nearby Telegraph Creek. She had grown up practically in the wilderness, setting out her first trapline at age five. She had a powerful .357-magnum pistol strapped to her side. "I never go anywhere without it," she said. "I've had eight bear scares in my life and had to kill two of the bears. Of course," she added, "I don't like to do that."

As I was standing getting acquainted with the geologists, a Stone's sheep topped the anticline and stood calmly regarding us from 30 yards away. The students scurried for their cameras, and the ram posed nicely, stepping carefully among the rocks, pausing to stick out his little black tongue and flick his tail. Now and then he made a little coughing snort. When the ram wandered away, I settled down to watch Tip at work. He knelt on the ground and methodically clawed rocks from a stratum with his hammer. He would whack each rock a solid blow, and regard with interest the fossil that was nearly always revealed when the rock split.

"There's a species of ammonite called *dayiceroides* that's found only in Portugal, here in the western parts of Canada, and in the western U. S.," Tip explained as he worked. "We geologists theorize that there was once a water connection from Portugal through the Caribbean to here. We have known *dayiceroides* was here; right now, I'm trying to find out what was living here with him." Whack.

Ammonites, the fossil shells of ancient mollusks, are useful creatures for dating rocks, Tip explained. "They're extinct second cousins of the *Nautilus*," he said. "They evolved rapidly and this species lived a relatively short time, only about a million years. So whenever you find them you get a good reliable date somewhere in the Lower Jurassic—about 180 million years ago."

As Tip went on working, an unexpected episode interrupted us. Tip and the students were scattered along the slopes of a small ravine, down which clucked a mother grouse and her four chicks. Suddenly two horsemen—a hunter and a guide—rode up to the opposite edge of the ravine, maybe 20 yards away.

"You mind if we shoot a ram here?" called the guide.

We gaped at him. Shoot a ram?

"Would you all please get down?" the guide said to us.

Wondering what was going on, we sidled out of the way and knelt. The guide held the horses while the hunter sprawled on his stomach and aimed his rifle over our heads. Blam! I scrambled with them over the anticline to near where our ram had posed. The hunter had his trophy, though a poor one, according to the guide.

"This animal was dying," he said, as he skinned and dressed it. "It's riddled with parasites. And look how bloated its stomach is.

If it had been healthy, it never would have been hanging around so close to you people."

Just west of our camp in Spatsizi was Mount Edziza Park, smaller than Spatsizi, but perhaps more dramatic. Here you can practically see the land abuilding. Vents around the 9,143-foot peak of Mount Edziza have erupted within the last 1,400 years, barely a millisecond ago geologically. Lava and cinder beds around the peak are a mile thick. One evening we climbed 600-foot-high Coffee Crater, so named for its rich brown color, as a full moon rose above the stark black-and-white lava flows. It was like scrambling up an enormous pile of cinders. Mount Edziza has erupted, geologists say, roughly every thousand years for the last million years.

A few days later I flew over Eve Cone just after dawn. The cone is 500 feet tall, absolutely symmetrical, with a crater at the top that is a perfect circle. Its most recent eruption may have been within the last few hundred years. The sharp outline of the cone rises unexpectedly, like a boil, from the flat plain around it.

Outside the boundary of Mount Edziza Park is Telegraph Creek, the only settlement on the 335-mile-long Stikine River. The town boomed several times during the 19th-century gold rushes into the area, and it was to be a key relay point on a telegraph line from North America to Europe via the Bering Strait planned during the 1860s. The telegraph line came to nothing, however—the trans-Atlantic cable was completed first.

Telegraph Creek marks the upper end of the navigable section of the Stikine River. Raft trips to Wrangell, on the coast, usually begin near here. Above the town is the Grand Canyon of the Stikine, a wild, barely known gorge where sheer walls and awesome rapids have discouraged all but the bravest.

I made a memorable drive to Telegraph Creek from the south. A simple gravel road threads through hundreds of miles of forest, crossing dozens of little streams on no-nonsense, erector-set bridges. At a couple of places the road widened and leveled, and signs appeared at the side: No Parking—Emergency Landing Strip. The last hour—winding down to the river's edge at Telegraph Creek—was a hair-raising, white-knuckled pitch. The crumbling little road switchbacked down canyon walls right at my elbow, with nothing but treetops a thousand feet below.

At the Riversong Cafe, with the Stikine a lively pale green rushing along outside the door, I had a cheeseburger and eavesdropped on townsfolk chatting of wedding showers, ice cream, and a pair of dams that B. C. Hydro hopes to build in their canyon.

"They want to flood the canyon before anyone really knows what's in there," I heard one woman say. If the dams are built, the resulting pair of back-to-back lakes would reach 50 miles upstream, necessitate the moving of a highway, and flood a new three-million-dollar railway bridge that has yet to be connected to a railroad. British Columbia, like the rest of the world, needs power.

THE FARTHER NORTH WE WENT in Canada, it seemed to me, the younger became the pilots. We had one helicopter pilot in Mount Edziza whose feet would barely reach the pedals. Another young fellow, flying us over a thousand square miles of ice and rock in Kluane National Park, suddenly slapped the map he had been studying,

On a barren, windblown peak in the White Goat Wilderness Area, two bighorn ewes and a lamb scramble up a rocky defile (opposite, top). Nearly all animals in the wild constantly position themselves so they can escape danger. A cow moose (opposite, lower) feeds in the shallow Cline River in White Goat; it will instantly take to the forest if alarmed. Among the other animals that inhabit the 171-square-mile wilderness area: goats, caribou, wolves, mountain lions, coyotes, elk, and grizzly bears, as well as more than a hundred species of birds.

and exclaimed triumphantly, "*Now* I know where we are."

In the Yukon, scheduled flights—what Canadians call "the Sked"—are informal affairs. The pilot may look like the boy who bags groceries at your neighborhood supermarket, and the flight attendant may be wearing jeans and a down jacket. The "Fasten Seat Belts" sign may stay lit the entire flight, yet the attendant still makes her little speech about oxygen masks and emergency exits.

It's a fairly short hop north from Telegraph Creek to Kluane National Park, but Kluane is in the Yukon, and the Yukon is a far country indeed. There's one telephone book of a hundred or so pages for the entire territory. ("Look at this," said Sam. "There are more taxidermists in Dawson than taxi companies.") Hitchhikers sprout like bearded weeds along the roadsides, and the Sked goes nearly everywhere. At Mayo, population 398, a young girl was picking wild flowers alongside the airstrip. "What do people do in Mayo?" I asked. "They work in the mines or they work in the bar." "Which do you do?" "Both." At Inuvik, far north in the Northwest Territories, there were Japanese businessmen, nuns, and a pilot I'd last seen at Whitehorse.

Kluane National Park—at 8,500 square miles more than half the size of Switzerland—is tucked into the southwest corner of the Yukon. Kluane is so remote and inaccessible that 90 percent of its features are still unnamed. It contains part of the St. Elias Mountains, Canada's highest range. Ten peaks exceed 15,000 feet, and the highest, Mount Logan, is 19,520 feet. All but burying these enormous mountains is the largest ice field in the world outside the polar areas. Down the flanks of the mountains slide 2,050 glaciers. From the air the region looks like solid, snow-covered ice, out of which black and jagged peaks emerge.

There are seven species of large mammals and 28 smaller species in the St. Elias Mountains, a rare richness this far north. Flying in Kluane, we saw a grizzly bear running across a river bottom, each step raising a little puff of dust. Some 180 species of birds have been found in the park, from redwing blackbirds to lesser yellowlegs. More than 700 kinds of flora—shrubs, trees, ferns, grasses—grow here, spreading across a wide range of climatic zones.

One bird, the wandering tattler, performs one of those mystifying feats of migration that so confound the imagination. Kluane's tattlers winter thousands of miles away in the South Pacific then return not only to the park but to the same clumps of dwarf willow, along the same streams, that they left the previous fall.

We camped in Kluane at the foot of the Donjek Glacier, where it spills down out of its valley. Its surface, as tossed and heaved as a bag of spilled marshmallows, held dozens of tiny but deep pools of astonishingly blue water. Our campsite resembled a World War I battlefield. Piles of rubble, left behind by the glacier, created ridges that stretched across the valley and stairstepped downward.

The Donjek River foamed and tumbled down the valley. I waded a couple of its tributaries, knee-deep in gray water that had been ice only a few minutes before; it was so cold I ached to the top of my head. Little clumps of sweet pea grew here and there, and whiffs of sage were wafted by the breeze. Ground squirrels stood on the slopes, their little hands in front of their mouths in a sort of "Oh my gosh!" stance as we walked past. Moose *(Continued on page 188)*

Lasting longer than summer, a snow patch survives into August in Spatsizi Plateau Wilderness Park. Osborn caribou seek its cool air for relief from insects. Caribou hooves suit most situations. Sharp edges provide good footing on rocks or ice; scoop-shaped undersides help the animals dig through snow for food; broad bottoms act as snowshoes in deep snow and as paddles in water. Seemingly bemused, a mountain goat (right) pauses in Spatsizi. Clumps of winter fur, which the goat sheds in spring, still cling to its side.

Full moon ghosts above a monochromatic landscape in Mount Edziza Park. These snow-spotted lava

beds and cinder cones grew from volcanic eruptions occurring as recently as a few hundred years ago.

Heaved and cracked by a narrowing valley, Kaskawulsh Glacier sweeps past jagged peaks in 8,500-square-mile Kluane National Park, in the southwestern corner of the Yukon Territory. The largest ice fields outside the polar regions sprawl here, and more than 2,000 glaciers—some of them juggernauts built of snow that fell during the last ice age—rumble down out of the mountains. Inside the park rise numerous peaks of the St. Elias Mountains, Canada's highest range. Ten of the peaks exceed 15,000 feet, including Mount Logan, highest of the high at 19,520 feet. Just outside Kluane, a bald eagle (left) comes to a precarious rest at the top of a spruce tree.

Twin arms of Kaskawulsh Glacier join to form a massive freeway of ice in Kluane Park. The huge

glacier—45 miles long—creates its own climate: Near-continuous winds howl down its length.

Moonglow bathes a caribou rack and skull in Spatsizi Park. Because Canada's thousands of caribou shed their horns each year, the north seems to sprout abandoned antlers everywhere. The attached partial skull indicates this animal lost its life—perhaps to old age, disease, or a predatory grizzly.

tracks dried in the mud alongside the streams. The face of the glacier, a dirty wall of ice a mile or so behind our camp, dripped and dribbled in the afternoon sun. The clatter of rocks released from the thawing ice echoed like shots off the mountainsides. I touched the glacier's face—cold, wet, solid. In the valley, black-and-white magpies chattered in a grove of spruce.

Between seven and eight thousand years ago, a group of hunters camped on a bluff near where the Alaska Highway now crosses the Aishihik River. The bits and pieces of bones and rock chips they left behind are some of the earliest evidence of mankind found in the Kluane region. Canoeing down the Kathleen River just outside the park, I passed the cabin of an elderly Indian woman who may very well have descended from those early hunters.

"Marge Jackson lives there," I was told later. "She's 63 and lives alone all winter, trapping mink." I looked her up and found her at a fishing camp a few miles south of Haines Junction. In her cozy log cabin she gave me a cup of tea and talked briefly, in heavily accented English, of her life. Her toddler granddaughter grinned from her high chair as she munched on a piece of bread smeared with jam.

"When did you learn English?" I asked Marge.

"I don't know," she said. "Maybe 1939, I reckon. First time I see a car, in maybe 1925, I think it was a big snake. My friend and me, we cry. It makes a big noise, you know? *We* don't know. Two men get out, try to talk to us. We don't know what they mean."

The little granddaughter had gone to sleep, face downward in her gooey lunch, her arms hanging at her sides. She looked dead. Marge woke her, washed her face, and put her to bed.

I asked Marge if she got lonely, living by herself all winter 30 miles from the nearest neighbor. "Lonely! How you get lonely when so much work to do?" She sets out four or five traplines of 20 to 30 traps each. "You go with me maybe! You see how lonely *you* get."

A few weeks later, at Old Crow, several hundred miles north, I found archaeologists at work looking for further evidence of early man in the Americas. Sponsored by the National Museum of Man and other institutions, scientists in several disciplines—archaeology, paleobotany, geology—were camped in tents a few miles up the Porcupine River from Old Crow. They had been there all summer.

In the radio tent Dr. Richard E. Morlan, bearded and brawny, explained the work to me. "There are a couple of hundred places here in the Old Crow basin that we're investigating," he said. "We're digging in bluffs of ancient sediment along the river and also in modern river bars. After all, you have to understand modern landscapes to understand ancient ones.

"We presume people entered the New World across the Bering Strait at one time or another." Previously, the earliest date for this migration was believed to be 27,000 years ago, but Dr. Morlan has a find that he thinks will push the date back much further. "We have found mammoth bones 80,000 years old that were fresh when they were fractured," Dr. Morlan explained. "Mammoth bones are very strong, very difficult to break. I think people were responsible for breaking them. Also, there's the appearance of cut marks that we think were made by stone tools on the bones. It happens when you're butchering an animal and your stone knife hits the bone. These are showing up in the 80,000-year-old level, too."

I had passed through Old Crow earlier in the summer, with a group of river rafters. We were headed north, to the end of the cordillera. The Firth River, which rises in the Davidson Mountains just across the border in Alaska, winds for 95 miles across the northwestern corner of the Yukon before emptying into the Beaufort Sea near Herschel Island. A Vancouver outfitter, Hyak River Expeditions, had put together a raft trip down the Firth—the first ever, as far as we could find out—and Sam and I had signed up to go along.

The logistics of the trip were complex. We all met at Whitehorse—seventeen men and two women—and piled aboard a chartered DC-3, a workhorse with its work cut out for it. We made a short flight to Dawson, on the banks of the Yukon River, and put down on a gravel strip. Like a mobile strike force, we pitched our tents in the tall grass behind the parked plane, and in the morning, after breakfast and a tour of the wooden sidewalks of Dawson, flew on north to Old Crow. Another gravel strip, a huddle of log houses, a clutch of Indian children watching us with friendly black eyes.

Here, above the Arctic Circle, we first encountered a phenomenon that would stay with us during our entire ten days on the Firth: no darkness. The sun never set, only dipped toward the horizon. The light at 3 a.m. was often brighter than at a cloudy noon. Photos taken at midnight have shadows as hard-edged as those in pictures snapped at breakfast.

A different plane was to fly us on north to the Firth. Our new pilot, Rick Nielsen, arrived at Old Crow at midnight in a single-engine Otter equipped with floats for landing on the nearby Porcupine. Rick would ferry us—five at a time—the 87 miles to Margaret Lake, which is just a couple of hundred yards from the banks of the Firth. Another of those boyish pilots who looked as if he ought to be

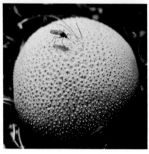

Lighting up in self-defense, the author fights fire—a blitz of mosquitoes—with smoke while seated on a hilltop in the northern Yukon. The insects here lived up to their fearsome reputation. One of the creatures (above) alights on a two-inch-wide puffball, a type of fungus.

home delivering papers, Rick loaded the first of our group aboard, and with a roar we swept down the Porcupine and lifted off. We flew over Old Crow Flats, an enormous expanse of hundreds of cheek-by-jowl lakes and ponds that glinted in the dusky light like puddles of spilled mercury. Little creeks zigzagged between them.

Rick circled mountains, probing for breaks in the low-lying clouds. At one point we became a blip on someone's radar screen; we were on the edge of the continent, where watch is constantly kept for unfriendly missiles. Rick maneuvered as instructed and identified us. A fellow pilot has photographs, Rick told us later, of glowing jet afterburners disappearing in the darkness—from military planes that had flown out of Fairbanks to look him over.

We picked up the scraggly headwaters of the Firth, braided and confused as they wound steeply down out of the mountains. The Firth is born in puddles and air and ice. Sheets of *aufeis*, pale blue, highly aerated ice, obscured the river here and there. We landed at Margaret Lake, half a mile long and a quarter of a mile wide, just as a whistling swan took off. For a few lovely moments it flew with long graceful sweeps beside us, just outside my window.

The Firth, pale and clear and very cold, was a short hike across hummocky tundra. Plovers stalked among the puffy cotton grass and alpine wild flowers. It took Rick the rest of the night to finish ferrying in the group, and about the time he finished, the clouds came down and it began to snow. Soggy flakes the size of hickory nuts coated the tundra, the tents, the mountains around us.

"Wind, cold," my notebook says of the next day, when we set off downriver through a wide valley edged by gently sloping tundra. The water was shallow and cold—33 degrees. Eagles fought in the air overhead—a mature and a young bald eagle collided and somersaulted. One dropped a fish, and the other came fluttering down to retrieve it. During the following days we wended steadily northward. I felt a hint of the excitement early explorers must have known. Each day brought unexpected scenes, every bend in the river led to an unknown. Ashore, I felt I was walking where perhaps no man had ever walked, seeing sights no man had seen. We had fresh grayling for breakfast and fed scraps to friendly gulls. The valley narrowed, and steeper slopes of tundra and rock rose alongside us. The rapids were fast and frequent, but not dangerous.

One day was filled with omens. I awoke to my 43rd birthday, having dreamt in the night of my grandfather's death; we were to enter the Firth's canyon that day, a 25-mile stretch of unknown rapids flanked by sheer 150-foot walls; I was in a raft with a skull and crossbones painted on its bow; just after setting off we passed a scrubby little spruce tree with a piece of black fabric dangling from a branch, borne there from who knows where.

But the day turned into the high point of my summer. The rapids were great sport, though one passenger was catapulted from the back of his raft, bounced as if on a trampoline into the water. The canyon walls beside us were twisted and folded, bent and broken. Some of the rock was a pale lavender. There were tilted slabs of dark shale, and chunks of granite, curved rocks, and jagged boulders. Little birds flitted around the dry beds of intermittent streams, where clumps of purple lupine grew. That night we celebrated my birthday and, seated around the campfire in the eerie light, read from the wilderness poetry of Robert Service.

From our campsite the next day, I looked to the top of a bluff a hundred yards away. There, plodding in our direction with a pigeon-toed amble, was a grizzly bear. He swung his head toward us, and I felt his gaze connect with mine. As naturalist Annie Dillard once wrote of a sight that stunned her: "It was less like seeing than like being for the first time seen, knocked breathless by a powerful glance." Even from a distance, before the bear turned and wandered off, I could feel the intensity of his curiosity.

Somewhere in the canyon, we crossed the tree line, and the little scrubby black spruce trees gave up and disappeared. Near the end of the Firth it occurred to me that, just as house cats often purr as they die, so most rivers relax and go calmly to their deaths. We floated out of the canyon onto the Arctic Coastal Plain, and looked back at the end of the cordillera. The mountains subsided into the tundra as if exhausted from the long journey north they had made.

We climbed a knoll, a solitary hump in miles of flat tundra, and looked north. The land disappeared, and a bank of clouds hung over the Beaufort Sea. The river widened and braided, then widened again to become a delta. Channels ran through a bed of ice three feet thick. At a lunch stop we huddled and stamped our feet to keep warm as the boatmen searched for a channel that would take us to the sea. The current slowed and died, the river became shallower, and we found ourselves outside the rafts, pulling them through ankle-deep water.

The ice ended and we were in the middle of a five-mile-wide delta. It was midnight. Still that eerie light stayed with us. The tide went out and we stood by our grounded rafts, our world a wide and empty one. Four or five miles ahead we could see the little spit of land that runs across the mouth of the Firth. The river's banks were far away on either side of us. We loaded what we needed for the night on our backs and made for shore.

Whistling swans honked and soared above the tundra. Their floating, graceful landings were almost too beautiful to watch. Snow buntings, little tuxedoed birds I had last seen on Mount Katahdin in Maine, hunted and pecked among the wild flowers.

The next day, tugging and rowing, we made it to the spit. Beyond it the ocean was thick with chunks of ice the size of easy chairs. The pieces moved, armada-like, eastward in the breeze. The shore was lined with tons of driftwood, pale trees washed clean by the pounding they had taken. It snowed again as we waited on the spit for the plane that was to pick us up. Heavy damp flakes coated everything. I strolled on the beach, picking up rocks. A seal peered from behind a chunk of ice. A flock of ducks startled me, the sudden *whuf whuf whuf* of their wings coming from behind. Arctic terns wheeled overhead.

As I faced north, with nothing but ice and water between me and the North Pole, I mused on wilderness. Wilderness is cold baths and solitude, I thought. Wilderness is hot oatmeal in the morning and sun in the afternoon. Wilderness is river-cooled feet, chipmunks, cheese and crackers with friends, and rain puddles on your plate. Wilderness is a magnet, irresistible. "I wish to speak a word for Nature," wrote Thoreau, "for absolute freedom and wildness."

Wilderness is freedom.

Frigid water pours aboard a raft as it surges through rapids of the Firth River, in the northern tip of the Yukon Territory. Jim Lavalley, co-owner of Hyak River Expeditions, muscles the craft through the white water, while Ivar Grimba, a Toronto stockbroker, hangs on. The author and the photographer joined Lavalley, Grimba, and 15 others for a trip down the Firth, a short but powerful river born in the Davidson Mountains in Alaska. The river threads a narrow canyon for 25 miles before descending to the Arctic Coastal Plain, then emptying into the Beaufort Sea. Grizzly bears and caribou haunt the riverbanks, and whistling swans and arctic terns nest on the spongy tundra. Even in July, the Arctic can assert itself: Fresh snow dusts peaks above Joe Creek, a tributary of the Firth (left), and ice slowly melts on cinquefoil blossoms (right).

Pointing toward an ominous sky, a grassy knoll juts above the flat arctic plain near the mouth of the Firth River. Finding evidence of kill sites at the knoll's base, archaeologists think ancient hunters once used it as a lookout for sighting game. At low tide (right), rafters wade ankle-deep in the Firth's delta beside their grounded rafts. A pencil-line spit on the horizon marks the northern edge of mainland Canada's wilderness lands; beyond the spit—the icy expanse of the Beaufort Sea.

Notes on Contributors

SAM ABELL has worked as a contract photographer for the National Geographic Society for 12 years. He has photographed two Special Publications, *The Pacific Crest Trail* and *Still Waters, White Waters*, and has contributed chapters to five others. In addition to this and his work for NATIONAL GEOGRAPHIC, Sam teaches photography and exhibits his color photographs in galleries throughout North America. He lives near Charlottesville, Virginia, with his wife, Denise.

JAMES CONAWAY is the author of two novels, *The Big Easy* and *World's End*, and two works of nonfiction, *Judge: The Life and Times of Leander Perez* and *The Texans*. He has published articles in many magazines, including *The Atlantic* and the *New York Times Magazine*, and has worked for several newspapers in the United States and in Europe. He was a Wallace Stegner Creative Writing Fellow at Stanford University and the recipient of an Alicia Patterson Fellowship in journalism to write about energy development. He is currently a writer for the *Washington Post Magazine*.

Photographs by RICHARD A. COOKE III have appeared in NATIONAL GEOGRAPHIC and in the Society's Book for World Explorers, *Amazing Animals of the Sea*. He has done free-lance assignments for TIME-LIFE wilderness books, *Outside* magazine, and *Sports Afield*, and in 1982 he completed a book on Molokai for a Canadian publisher. Rik has held several gallery shows of his work. He lives in Eugene, Oregon.

LOUIS DE LA HABA has traveled widely in the Americas, Europe, and the Middle East. A wilderness enthusiast, he has been associated with the National Geographic Society as a staff member or as a free-lance writer since 1963. His contributions to Special Publications include chapters in *America's Magnificent Mountains*, *Trails West*, and other books. He is a graduate of Amherst College and holds an M.A. degree in anthropology from George Washington University.

Iowa-born RON FISHER joined the Special Publications staff in 1966. His assignments have dealt largely with the North American wilderness. He is the author of *The Appalachian Trail*, which appeared in 1972, and *Still Waters, White Waters*, a book on canoeing published in 1977. He has contributed chapters to a number of other Special Publications and, when not writing, has served as managing editor for several more.

Photographer STEPHEN J. KRASEMANN has completed several free-lance assignments for NATIONAL GEOGRAPHIC and various Special Publications during the past three years. Stephen has also done fashion photography and once toured with the Rolling Stones rock group as their publicity photographer. His work has appeared in many magazines, including *Audubon*, *Natural History*, *National Wildlife*, and *GEO*. A U. S. citizen, Stephen lives near Thunder Bay, Ontario.

YVA MOMATIUK and JOHN EASTCOTT, a wife-and-husband team, have photographed and written about many remote parts of the world. Born and educated in Warsaw, Poland, Yva holds a degree in architecture. John, a New Zealander, received his degree in photographic arts in London. Journeys to the Arctic resulted in a book—*Great Slave Lake Blues*—for a Canadian publisher, and "Still Eskimo, Still Free: The Inuit of Umingmaktok" for the November 1977 NATIONAL GEOGRAPHIC. In 1979 Yva and John contributed a chapter to the Special Publication *Exploring America's Backcountry*.

THOMAS O'NEILL was born in Ohio and grew up in Champaign, Illinois. A graduate of Beloit College, he joined the Society's staff in 1976 and has since traveled to Italy, Australia, and 46 states while on assignment for Special Publications. He is the author of *Back Roads America* and has contributed to several other books.

PAUL VON BAICH studied photography at the Vienna Institute of Arts in Austria. Since moving to Canada in 1960, he has received a Canada Arts Council Award to photograph the Arctic and has contributed to a number of Canadian and U. S. publications. His work has also appeared in the book *Between Friends/Entre Amis*, produced by the National Film Board of Canada. Since 1976 Paul has published five books of photography, including his latest, *Light in the Wilderness*, in 1981. He lives near Campbellford, Ontario.

WAYNE LANKINEN

Tiny jewel in the crown of Canada's vast wilderness lands, Peyto Lake shimmers below snowcapped Rocky Mountain peaks in Banff National Park, in western Alberta. Bright red blossoms of Indian paintbrush color the foreground. Oldest park in Canada, Banff dates to 1885.

Composition for *Canada's Wilderness Lands* by National Geographic's Photographic Services, Carl M. Shrader, Chief, Lawrence F. Ludwig, Assistant Chief. Printed and bound by Holladay-Tyler Printing Corp., Rockville, Md. Color separations by the Lanman Progressive Company, Washington, D. C.; Lincoln Graphics, Inc., Cherry Hill, N. J.; NEC, Inc., Nashville, Tenn.

Library of Congress CIP Data

Main entry under title:

Canada's wilderness lands.

Bibliography: p.
Includes index.
1. Northwest, Canadian—Description and travel—1981-
____. 2. Maritime Provinces—Description and travel. I.
National Geographic Society (U. S.). Special Publications
Division.
F1060.92.C28   917.2   81-48074
ISBN 0-87044-413-1 (regular binding)   AACR2
ISBN 0-87044-418-2 (library binding)

Index

Acknowledgments

The Special Publications Division is grateful to the individuals, organizations, and agencies named or quoted in the text and to those cited here for their generous assistance: Fred Alt, Charles D. Arnold, Fred Bamber, Thomas Barry, Jacques Bertrand, Richard Bill, Tony Boles, Boreal Institute for Northern Studies, Ian Campbell, Ray Chipeniuk, F. G. Cooch, M. J. Pierre De-Grandmont, Ross Dobson, M. H. Estabrooks, Brian Garbett, Willis J. Gertsch, Nicholas Gessler, J. M. Gillett, Douglas R. Grant, Joel Grendjambe, Fred Gudmundson, Larry Hagen, Charles O. Handley, Jr., Ellen Henderson, George Hobson, Hudson's Bay House Library, Moira Irvine, Hope Johnson, Kerry R. Joy, James D. Keyser, Job Kuijt, Ernie Kuyt, Labrador Institute of Northern Studies, Lucie Lagueux, Herbert Levi, Bob Lewis, Fred E. Lockhart, J. J. McClelland, Jr., John McGlynn, Bill McIntyre, J. Ross Mackay, Pamela Mackay, June Markwart, James G. Mead, Claude Mondor, Chris Morrison, Dalton Muir, W. T. Munro, Joe Ohokannoak, Gerald Osborn, Leonard Petroski, Ross Peyton, George F. Russell III, Susan Sawyer, George W. Scotter, Arnet Sheppard, Norman Simmons, Silver Smoliak, Jim Stomp, Stephen Suddes, Terrain Sciences Division of the Geological Survey of Canada, Frank T'Seleie, John Walper, George E. Watson, Pete Weddell, Cleve Wershler, Stephen Zoltai.

Additional Reading

The reader may wish to consult the National Geographic Society Index for articles, and to refer to the following books: A. W. F. Banfield, *The Mammals of Canada*; H. P. Biggar, *The Voyages of Jacques Cartier*; Max Braithwaite, *The Western Plains*; George Frederick Clarke, *Six Salmon Rivers and Another*; John Robert Colombo, *Canadian References*; R. J. W. Douglas (editor), *Geology and Economic Minerals of Canada*; Moira Dunbar and Keith R. Greenaway, *Arctic Canada from the Air*; E. W. Hawkes, *The Labrador Eskimo*; T. H. McDonald (editor), *Exploring the Northwest Territory*; David N. Nettleship and Pauline A. Smith (editors), *Ecological Sites in Northern Canada*; Frederick Pratson, *A Guide to Atlantic Canada*; Franklin Russell, *The Atlantic Coast*; Robert P. Sharp, *Glaciers*; David A. E. Spalding (editor), *A Nature Guide to Alberta*; Vilhjálmur Stéfansson, *The Stéfansson-Anderson Arctic Expedition*; Robert Stewart, *Labrador*; David E. Sugden and Brian S. John, *Glaciers and Landscapes*; John Theberge (editor), *Kluane, Pinnacle of the Yukon*; John Peter Turner, *The North-West Mounted Police, 1873-1893*; John Warkentin (editor), *Canada, A Geographical Interpretation*; George Whalley, *The Legend of John Hornby*; Roger Wilson (editor), *The Land That Never Melts, Auyuittuq National Park*.